THE POLITICS OF GOD

THE POLITICS OF GOD

The Rise and Rise of Political Religion

TP O'Mahony

VERITAS

Published 2023 by
Veritas Publications
7–8 Lower Abbey Street
Dublin 1
Ireland

publications@veritas.ie
www.veritas.ie

ISBN 978 1 80097 040 3

10 9 8 7 6 5 4 3 2 1

A catalogue record for this book is available from the British Library.

Thank you to the *Daily Telegraph*, the *Guardian*, the *Irish Examiner*, the *Irish
Times*, the *Times*, the *Sydney Morning Herald*, Cruxnow.com and the Pew
Research Center for granting permission to Veritas Publication to reproduce
article extracts. *Every effort was made to contact the copyright holders of material
reproduced. If any infringement has occurred, the owners of such copyright are
requested to contact the publishers.*

Cover designed by Padraig McCormack, Veritas Publications
Designed by Jeannie Swan, Veritas Publications
Typeset by Clare Meredith, Veritas Publications
Printed in the Republic of Ireland by SprintPrint, Dublin

Veritas Publications is a member of Publishing Ireland.

*Veritas books are printed on paper made from the wood pulp of managed forests.
For every tree felled, at least one tree is planted, thereby renewing natural resources.*

In memory of my wife

Elizabeth O'Mahony

1939–2021

Contents

Foreword

In the Western democracies the historically fierce grip of religiously inspired and deeply embedded conservative values claiming divine legitimacy, including misogyny and homophobia, has finally loosened. They were so pervasive and persuasive that it was easy to lose sight of their religious origins for they outcropped everywhere and still do in many jurisdictions in civil laws as well as in seemingly temporal attitudes, practices and perspectives. Make no mistake however the major faith systems of the world, adhered to by five out of seven of the world's population and dominated firstly by Christianity and secondly by Islam, and which are growing exponentially in Africa and Asia while dwindling in the West, are today, as they have been for centuries, the most effective carriers and validators of the intolerance and extremism which wreak havoc across our planet, hubristically holding back progress, blocking potential, wasting lives and too often silencing opponents and critics.

In most of the West, thanks to massified second- and third-level education and a surge in national and international human rights treaties, structures and discourse, the intellectual freedoms of speech, conscience, thought and belief have begun to dismantle the centuries old infrastructure of unheavenly bigotry, hatred, control, intolerance and fanaticism born out of venerated holy books and hugely influential faith systems which simultaneously claim when challenged to be sources of love, tolerance and human dignity. Traditional faith systems are under pressure in the West and are finding it difficult to withstand the onslaught of an educated laity who no longer believe as they were once (and often still are) taught they are born or initiated by baptism or other forms of initiation into faith systems from which they cannot disengage. Membership for example of the world's biggest Christian denomination, the Catholic Church, is based, according to the Church's canon law, on the groundless notion that baptismal promises create permanent obligations of obedience to the teaching of the Church's bishops. For 84 per cent of Church membership those promises are entirely fictitious since they were made not by but on behalf of non-sentient infants on the occasion of their baptism, when they were simply and obviously incapable of giving consent to such a massive negation of their fundamental rights to freedom of religion, conscience, thought and opinion. Today many walk away from the churches and other faith systems not because they are apostates or schismatics or heretics as many faiths would insist, not because they are seduced by the lure of superficial secularism but rather because they are certain they are entirely free to make up their own minds about what to believe. Ireland, after a long period of Catholic Church moral and legal domination, is now a leading light in that freedom walk.

This is an age-old battle. For as long as there have been people and religions there have also been politics, woven into the warp and weft of faith lives. Today is no different as TP O'Mahony shows here in his commentary on the often dangerous rise and rise of religious politics worldwide. The difference today is that the battles for full acceptance of progressive, liberal values in the educated West is far from over. There is strong evidence of pushback, of illiberal regrouping, of fresh religious aggression designed to take us back to the past, to make the future as dark a place as that past was and is for so many human beings.

Religious leaders across the world are their own worst enemies thanks to their signal failure to engage in meaningful dialogue on the basis of gender, ethnic and racial equality as well as religious respect and parity of esteem. If, as TP says, 'A fundamentalist, theocratic and misogynist administration with a hard-line belief in global jihad was now ruling Afghanistan', it has a litany of parallels throughout distant and recent history. Only a century and a half ago Pope Pius IX, then both a spiritual head and political head of the vast Papal States which were held so often by awful violence (just as the Reformation/English colonisation was imposed in Ireland by awful violence), tried to convince the world that God intended the entire world to be spiritually and temporally ruled by the pope, that individual human rights were anathema and obedience to the Magisterium was a divine command to all. If he had had the military might to impose that view, which mercifully he did not, then a different twentieth century history might have been written. But what he could not see and what the jihadists and other religious fanatics of varying degrees cannot see is that their day is not coming. It is over. The battle for the human rights and fundamental freedoms of individual human beings is the battle of our time and we are now better equipped than at any other time in the history of humanity to engage and to win. With international institutions like the United Nations, with international treaties, with the great bulwark that is the European Union, we are organised as never before to protect democracy and push towards a future where there will be the full flowering of human dignity. The better we make them work effectively despite their weaknesses, the more we develop robust solidarity around shared values and principles rooted in mutual tolerance and respect, the quicker that future will arrive, the quicker we will drain the oxygen from the conduits of intolerance. The world's faith systems have to decide what side of that divide they want to find themselves on. Can they navigate towards each other in humble generosity and willingness to compromise, filling in history's vacuums and chasms of ignorance where bad things fester, for which they must take responsibility? Or will they do what they have traditionally done, take the moral high ground from which they see only the mote in the other's eye and not the beam in their own, while carefully crafting endless interfaith, ecumenical photo opportunities and committees that move in cynical circles that make glacial headway? This book is a warning that should be heeded by all people of faith to conscientiously and conspicuously make faith work towards the creation and sustaining of a global culture of love, open-minded, inclusive, affirming of all God's creation.

I grew up in a determinedly Protestant jurisdiction within the United Kingdom which abjectly failed to do that though it was a place dominated by legions of Christian churches and where God was routinely invoked to justify the secular politics of bigotry, inequality and factional dominance. It led to violence and a wary grimness that never leaves the soul. There is a better way. A hard way, yes, as my homeland shows in the constant efforts of its weary majority who favour equality and partnership that tries to reconcile and live in a stable peace. Whether religion will play a noble part in finding that way is up to people of faith finding their voice within their own faith systems, critiquing them, challenging them to be sources of real goodness in the world, holding dysfunctional leadership accountable, liberating God's people and their energies to embrace one another across all the divides that hold us back from full, comfortable acceptance of the otherness of others. The tsunami of goodness across the European Union that spontaneously enveloped the tragic, uprooted people of Ukraine in the face of Putin's demonic evil, backed God help us by the Russian Orthodox Christian Patriarch Kirill, allows us to hope in and for the humanity of humanity and its eventual triumph. Sometime soon Lord please!

Dr Mary McAleese
President of Ireland, 1997–2011

Acknowledgements

The origins of this book can be traced directly to the terrible events of 9/11, which compelled a far-reaching reappraisal of the role of religion in the global order.

When I started work I had ample background material to draw on because some very distinguished authors, even way before 9/11, had explored aspects of 'political religion', and I am greatly indebted to them.

Despite all of this, I hit a difficult period and came close to abandoning the entire project. What re-energised me was the discovery in 2010 in a bookshop in Athens (visiting Greece was the fulfilment of a long-standing ambition) of a paperback edition of Madeleine Albright's book *The Mighty and the Almighty: Reflections on America, God, and World Affairs*.

At home I was blessed to have the support and encouragement of friends such as Tim Ryan, John Hayes, Pat Hannon, John Cooney and Margaret Mansfield, as well as my children Veronica and John.

I am especially grateful to our former president Mary McAleese for agreeing to write the foreword. And I am thankful also to Dr Maurice Manning, chancellor of the NUI, and Professor John Horgan for their endorsements.

It was Tim Ryan who first put me in touch with Michael Brennan, who liked the manuscript and recommended submitting it to Síne Quinn, publisher at Veritas. I was delighted when she accepted it for publication. I can recall my feeling of quiet satisfaction the morning I received her call.

In the bleak aftermath of my wife's death, finishing the book was, as it turned out, the best tribute to Elizabeth's memory.

The editing of the manuscript was in the capable hands of, first, Emma O'Donoghue, and then Leeann Gallagher. They did an excellent job, and working with them was a pleasure.

Cork, January 2023

Introduction

THE RETURN OF THE TALIBAN

If you don't understand religion,
including the abuse of religion,
you don't understand what is
happening in our world.

Lyse Doucet

In a pointedly symbolic act, the Taliban raised its flag – a white banner with a verse from the Qur'an in black printed on it – over the Afghan presidential palace in Kabul on the twentieth anniversary of the 9/11 attacks in New York and Washington DC. The flag-raising ceremony marked the official start of the all-male, all-Taliban (there had been speculation about an 'inclusive' administration) government. On the same day the Taliban also orchestrated a march of fully veiled women who filled an auditorium at Kabul University. This was seen as a well-orchestrated snub to the past twenty years of Western efforts to empower women. One of the first acts of the new government was to abolish the Ministry for Women's Affairs.

A month after the creation of the Islamic Emirate of Afghanistan, the *Guardian* carried this report: 'Women in Afghanistan will only be allowed to study at university in gender-segregated classrooms and Islamic dress will be compulsory, the Taliban have announced, stoking fears that gender apartheid will be imposed on the country.'[1]

---

1   *The Guardian*, 13 September 2021.

Before the fall of Kabul to the Taliban on 15 August 2021, universities across the country had been co-educational and women did not have to conform to any dress code. That quickly changed. A fundamentalist, theocratic and misogynist administration with a hardline belief in global jihad was now ruling Afghanistan.

'Women's rights will be subject to the Taliban's strict interpretation of Muslim canon law, Sharia,' Michael Jansen, a respected commentator on Islam, predicted just days after the fall of Kabul.[2]

Then came a report that a senior official, a man described as a 'veteran Taliban enforcer', had told the Associated Press (AP) that amputations of hands and executions for convicted criminals would resume in a return to their harsh version of Islamic justice. 'No one will tell us what our laws should be. We will follow Islam and we will make our laws on the Qur'an,' said Nooruddin Turabi, a member of the new government.[3]

Outside of some countries of the Middle East, notably Saudi Arabia and Iran, there is no more spectacular example of 'political theology' on display. Perhaps we should also mention the political implications and influence of Islam in Pakistan, Hinduism in India and Buddhism in Myanmar. And let us not forget how the Shinto religion was harnessed by Japan's ruling elite in the period 1930–45 to buttress militarism and imperial expansionist ambition in the build-up to and during World War II. The close relationship was such that some scholars refer to it as 'State Shinto'.

'Nowhere else in modern history do we find so pronounced an example of State sponsorship of a religion – in some respects the State can be said to have created Shinto as its official "tradition".'[4]

But it isn't just in the Islamic world and other places that this phenomenon manifests itself. Much nearer home we have seen it at work in Northern Ireland, with very deleterious effects. Before the establishment of that State in 1920, it was deeply embedded and influential in the culture and society of the Irish Free State after independence, and later, after the enactment of the 1937 Constitution, in the Irish Republic (though the formal declaration of a republic didn't occur until 1949).

---

2   *The Irish Times*, 21 August 2021.

3   *The Guardian*, 24 September 2021.

4   Helen Hardacre, *Shintō and the State, 1868–1988* (New Jersey: Princeton University Press, 1991), p. 3.

Irish public life and public affairs were dominated by 'political religion', specifically 'political Catholicism'; this forms the background to understanding the 'Church's monopoly over Irish morality', as Tom Inglis puts it in his excellent book *Moral Monopoly: The Rise and Fall of the Catholic Church in Modern Ireland*. Inglis, a lecturer in sociology in UCD, explained:

> In the heyday of the Catholic Church's power, particularly during the fifty years after the foundation of the State, its influence expanded beyond the religious field into the field of politics, economics, education, health, social welfare, the media and many other fields. The power of the Church meant that it structured not just the religious life of the Irish people, but their social, political and economic life as well. Consequently, the strategies through which Irish Catholics struggled to gain cultural, social, political and economic and cultural capital were linked in with living a good Catholic life.[5]

This has been reiterated by Anna Grzymala-Busse, professor of European and Eurasian studies at the University of Michigan:

> In the name of protecting the Irish nation, the Catholic Church was heavily involved in policing the moral and political spheres, and in fact argued successfully that the two were the same. Until the late twentieth century, the Church's authority was (literally) unquestioned.[6]

Grzymala-Busse had earlier explained how the fusion of religion with national identity had greatly enhanced the Church's power and influence.

> In Ireland, Catholicism was the core pillar of an Irish, as opposed to an English, identity, and the Church promoted the fusion of

---

5   Tom Inglis, *Moral Monopoly: The Rise and Fall of the Catholic Church in Modern Ireland* (Dublin: Dublin University Press, 1998) (2nd edn), pp. 245–6.

6   Anna Grzymala-Busse, *Nations Under God: How Churches Use Moral Authority to Influence Policy* (Princeton and Oxford: Princeton University Press, 2015), p. 65.

national and religious identities, especially in the nineteenth century. With the local priest serving numerous roles in the community, religion and its practices in Ireland were very much embedded in everyday social life and relations.[7]

The crucial link between religion and identity in Ireland was also explored at length and with great insight by historian Marianne Elliott, a native of Northern Ireland and former director of the Institute of Irish Studies at Liverpool University. The title of the book in which she did this could hardly be more apposite: *When God Took Sides*.

She reminds her readers that the 'association of Irishness with Catholicism has been common for a number of centuries', and then goes on to explain how Catholics became the 'real' Irish in common perception.

> As such, Irish nationalism (particularly its republican variety) is deluding itself by underplaying its exclusive and exclusionary religious roots and ethos. In this I see Irish nationalism as another form of religion in disguise, one of the many ethno-religious nationalisms which have come to remind the modern world of the continuing force of religious-based identities.[8]

In a wider historical context we have multiple examples of the role of 'political religion', some good, some morally repugnant. What are we to make, for instance, of a pope signing a treaty with a fascist dictator (Pius XI and Benito Mussolini in Rome), or an apostolic nuncio (who would go on the become Vatican secretary of state) regularly dining with a murderous tyrant (Angelo Sodano and General Augusto Pinochet in Santiago, Chile), or the head of the Russian Orthodox Church publicly supporting a ruthless autocrat (Kirill I and Vladimir Putin in Moscow)?

That unholy alliance between patriarch and president came into sharp focus after Putin's invasion of Ukraine in February 2022 shattered peace in Europe and threatened the safety of the entire world. 'The Orthodox

---

7   Ibid.

8   Marianne Elliott, *When God Took Sides: Religion and Identity in Ireland* (Oxford: Oxford University Press, 2009), pp. 20–1.

Patriarch of Moscow has put his religious authority at the service of the Russian President's unbridled nationalism,' the editor-in-chief of *La Croix*, Jérôme Chapuis, wrote at the time.[9]

And then there is the blending of politics and religion in Britain. The Church of England, established by King Henry VIII (in the process making himself the supreme governor – a title that passed to each succeeding monarch and is held today by King Charles III) is the established or State Church. Twenty-six of its bishops have seats and voting rights in the House of Lords, so they can scrutinise and vote on any piece of legislation. No other religion is afforded this privilege.

In contradistinction to these examples, we could cite numerous 'good' examples of how 'political religion' has worked to enrich the human condition. And we must never forget how religion can have a vital role in the promotion of peace and tolerance.

All popes, especially in modern times, are political actors by virtue of their office – some, of course, more than others. In this regard, the title of John Cornwell's 1999 biography of Pius XII is telling: *Hitler's Pope*. In the aftermath of the Industrial Revolution the great papal social encyclicals, beginning with Leo XIII's *Rerum novarum* in 1891 (which came to be known as 'The Workers' Charter'), have championed the centrality of human dignity and human rights, the pursuit of social justice, and provided humankind with a moral framework within which to evaluate the quest for a just society, the emergence of communism and socialism, the workings and effects of capitalism and, especially in John XXIII's great encyclical *Pacem in terris* (1963), reflections on relations between states, disarmament and the promotion of peace.

We are faced with almost daily evidence in newspapers, television and on social media platforms of the capacity of religion to do much good but also to do great harm. John Bowker, editor of the *Oxford Dictionary of World Religions*, has written a book on this, using the phrase the 'paradox of religions' to describe this dual effect. It is clear, he asserts, that religions 'in their beliefs, behaviours and institutions, are involved in much that is harmful. But at the same time they are involved in much that is extremely

---

9   *La Croix*, 22 March 2022.

good'.[10] Despite this 'paradox', Bowker is in no doubt about the persistence and relevance of religion in the modern world.

> If religions did not matter so much to so many people, they might well have disappeared long ago. But they do matter and they are still very much with us ... Back in 1985, I made this appeal: The entanglement of religions in virtually all the intransigent problems which confront and threaten us means that we must become more serious in the ways in which we try to understand the power of religious belief both for evil and for good ... One of the most obvious reasons why we seem to drift from one disastrous ineptitude to another is, ironically, that far too few politicians have read Religious Studies at a University. As a result, they literally do not know what they are talking about on almost any of the major international issues. They simply cannot. It is time we began to educate ourselves, not just in economics, or in politics, or in technology, but also in the dynamics of religious belief and continuity, because whether we like it or not, it is religion which still matters more than anything else to most people alive today.[11]

All of this is surely even more germane in the post-9/11 world where there is indisputable evidence of the impact of religion on global affairs. As Beverley Milton-Edwards, professor in the School of Politics, International Studies and Philosophy at Queen's University, Belfast, has pointed out: 'In the first two decades of the twenty-first century the phenomenon of Islamic fundamentalism remains one of the most significant issues in global politics, discourse and international relations.'[12]

---

10   John Bowker, *Religion Hurts: Why Religions Do Harm as Well as Good* (London: SPCK, 2018), p. 8.

11   Ibid., pp. 9–10.

12   Beverley Milton-Edwards, *Islamic Fundamentalism Since 1945* (London and New York: Routledge, 2014), p. 1.

Chapter 1

ALTAR AND THRONE

Throughout most of Christian history,
theories of the relationship between the
Church and the political have generally little to
do with the life and teachings of Jesus Christ.

Elizabeth Phillips

The cover of the G2 section of the *Guardian* was stark: against a black background the date was emblazoned in white numerals across the centre of the page – 11.09.2001 – and then under it these five words: THE DAY THE EARTH STOOD STILL.

Images of the shocking attacks on the World Trade Center in New York and the Pentagon in Washington DC will live forever in the memory of all those who witnessed them on television. Viewers could hardly believe what they were seeing.

The geopolitical consequences of those attacks have been immense and far-reaching. The earth may not have stood still on 9/11, but the terrible events of that day dramatically altered the way we look at the world today, at global affairs, and at religion in particular.

In her preface to the second edition of a 2009 book on world religions (which she edited), Linda Woodhead, professor of sociology of religion at Lancaster University, summed up the changed appreciation of religion:

When the first edition was sent to the publishers in early 2001, the subject of religion in the modern world was still considered marginal by many people. In the intervening years that situation has changed out of all recognition. Like it or loathe it, religion is back on the agenda again.

As the first edition showed, religion was a major force in the modern world well before 2001. Contrary to claims about recent religious resurgence, religion has not popped up like some jack-in-the-box. Rather, it has made itself known in ways which are harder to ignore. The attack on the World Trade Center on 11 September 2001 is the most obvious example, but other more incremental developments have also been important. These include global migrations which have brought religious pluralism to the heart of a supposedly secular Europe, the continuing growth of new forms of spirituality, and the reconfiguration of religion in a media culture.

What has changed the most is thus the way we look at religion, and how seriously we take it. Religion is no longer dismissed as a private pastime, but is taken more seriously as a public and political force. This change, in turn, impacts upon religion itself, often lending it new confidence and vitality, and increasing its range and power.[1]

Religion has now entered the global age, breaking down frontiers. It is now seen in many quarters – not least in policymaking circles in the world's major capitals – in a new light. More than ever before, religion is politically important today, and aspects of globalisation have undoubtedly contributed to this. According to Malory Nye, 'From the local to the global level, religion is – more than ever – an important and hotly debated part of modern life in the twenty-first century.'[2]

What 9/11 also did was reopen – with a new urgency – the old debate about religion and violence. This is a debate with a long pedigree; we need only think of the Crusades in the eleventh and twelfth centuries, and the 'wars of religion' that raged in the sixteenth and seventeenth centuries in

---

1   Linda Woodhead, *Religions in the Modern World: Traditions and Transformations* (London and New York: Routledge, 2009) (2nd edn), preface, p. xix.

2   Malory Nye, *Religion: The Basics* (London and New York: Routledge, 2008) (2nd edn), p. 21.

the aftermath of the Reformation. This is also a debate that has a particular pertinence to the Irish situation, as former BBC journalist Martin Dillon has graphically reminded us in his book, *God and the Gun*, which deals with the churches and terrorism in Ireland during a thirty-year period in Northern Ireland, a period scarred by paramilitary violence that lasted from 1968 until the Good Friday Agreement of 1998, during which over 3,500 people lost their lives.[3]

Mark Juergensmeyer of the University of California, in a preface to the paperback edition of his book exploring the global rise of religious violence, highlighted the central issue:

> Perhaps the first question that came to mind when television around the world displayed the extraordinary aerial assaults on the World Trade Center and the Pentagon on September 11, 2001, was why anyone would do such a thing. When it became clear that the perpetrators' motivations were couched in religious terms, the shock turned to anger. How could religion be related to such vicious acts?[4]

At first glance, any link between religion and violence seems incongruous. Yet since the 9/11 attacks the world has become acutely aware of what the novelist JG Ballard called the 'sinister fusion of religion and politics'.

For those of us accustomed to believe that religion is a force for good and a promoter of peace, and politics a means of creating a just and equal society, proof of the toxic and even lethal mix of the two has come as something of a shock.

This may be due to complacency, indifference or even ignorance on our part. Did too many of us in the West accept that religion was somehow 'neutral' when it came to politics, or that religion even occupied a separate sphere – and that ne'er the twain shall meet? Why would we ever think that religion might be 'political' or that politics would harness or exploit or subvert religion for its own ends?

---

3 Martin Dillon, *God and the Gun: The Church and Irish Terrorism* (New York: Routledge, 1999).
4 Mark Juergensmeyer, *Terror in the Mind of God: The Global Rise of Religious Violence* (California: University of California Press, 2001), preface, p. xi.

Chapter 2

QUEST FOR LEGITIMACY

We pose a terrible threat to our
religious freedoms – and therefore to
our democracy – when we try to keep
religious voices out of the public square.

Stephen L. Carter

It began, some would argue, after the Battle of the Milvian Bridge in AD 312, when Emperor Constantine, emerging victorious after fighting under the sign of the Cross (following instructions received in a dream), bestowed great favours on Christianity, making it in effect the official (State) religion of the Roman Empire. Attributing his victory to the Christian God, he forged a new alliance between Altar and Throne, between Church and State, marking the birth of political religion. As Alain de Botton put it colourfully, thanks to the victory of Constantine, Jesus became unwittingly 'the head of a gigantic, State-sponsored Christian Church.'[1]

The most modern – and extreme – manifestations of political religion in action are al-Qaeda and its offshoots and affiliates, Boko Haram, al-Shabaab and Isis (or Isil or Islamic State), and also the Taliban, though this movement is rooted in another branch of militant Islam known as Deobandism. All the others are rooted in Wahhabism (named after its founder, Muhammad

---

1   Alain de Botton, *Religion for Atheists: A Non-Believer's Guide to the Uses of Religion* (London: Hamish Hamilton, 2012), p. 298.

ibn Abd al-Wahhab), a fundamentalist, puritanical and militant version of Islam that is the official or State religion of Saudi Arabia. The Deobandis, however, share many of the beliefs of the Wahhabis.

The 'politicisation' of religion is almost as old as religion itself. Some would go so far as to say that the politicisation of religion has been consubstantial with religion itself. Rulers have always been cognisant of the importance of having religion on their side, not because of any innate regard for religion (at least not in all cases) but because of its utility value. Accordingly, over the centuries they have plotted and schemed and pursued associations and alliances to gain the advantages and benefits that would accrue from winning over religion.

Emperors, kings, princes, sultans, despots and tyrants have sought to harness, utilise, exploit and yoke religion for their own purposes, to advance their causes, to legitimise their regimes, to sanction their policies, or to pacify the masses.

Democratically elected leaders have also turned to religion with the aim of using it to bestow extra authority on the office of president or prime minister or taoiseach and to bolster their programmes for government, or to underpin and divinely enhance their constitutions and charters of rights. Conversely, down the ages, religious leaders – popes, patriarchs, archbishops, rabbis, ayatollahs and evangelical preachers – have shown a readiness to form alliances and pacts with states, governments, leaders of political movements and even dictatorships. The main aim of these arrangements is to enlist State aid and support for the protection and promotion of religious freedom and religious tolerance.

But these alliances were often entered into in the hope or with the intention that the State might confer privileged status on one particular religion above others, or in the expectation that the State might use its legislative apparatus to enforce a particular system of faith-based morality or even to favour a particular Church by ensuring that its ministers of religion would be exempt from State taxes or would receive State stipends. All of this was perhaps best summed up by the Greek-born film director Costa-Gavras who once said that if the Catholic Church has lasted for two thousand years this was because it has always been on the side of the powerful.[2]

---

2   Interview with Maya Jaggi for the *Guardian*, 4 April 2009.

Of course, to some the term 'political religion' will seem an oxymoron, or a contradiction in terms. Politics may be defined as the art or science of government, the practice or study of forming, directing and administering states or other political units, or, more narrowly, any activity concerned with the acquisition of power and gaining one's own ends. Religion, on the other hand, is more difficult to define. Here are two of the standard dictionary definitions:

1. 'A belief in God or gods; a system of worship and faith; a formalised expression of belief' (*Webster's English Dictionary*)
2. 'Belief in a superhuman controlling power, especially in a personal God or gods entitled to obedience and worship' (*Oxford Dictionary of Current English*)

One problem with these definitions is that they are theocentric; if we define religion as worship of a creator God who sustains the world, this still leaves a problem. It would cover theistic faiths, but not non-theistic traditions, and so would exclude Buddhism for example. 'A world faith without a belief in God, Buddhism opens up new and interesting ways of encountering religion focused on the Buddha's teaching that there exists an important relationship between mindful awareness and spiritual awakening,' according to David Torevell of Liverpool Hope University College.[3]

The links between religion and politics are very old. 'Religion and politics have been interconnected throughout history,' Jonathan Fox reminds us. 'For every ancient political entity for which we have records, religion was intimately connected to politics.'[4]

In today's world, Fox says that religion's influence on politics manifests itself through multiple and sometimes overlapping agencies. 'These include how governments address religion, the political activities of all sorts of religious groups and organisations, and religion's influence on society in general.'[5] For examples of the latter, we need only consider the long dominance of the Catholic Church in the Republic and the way this

---

3   Ian S. Markham and Tinu Ruparell, eds, *Encountering Religion: An Introduction to the Religions of the World* (Oxford: Blackwell, 2000), p. 190.
4   Jonathan Fox, *An Introduction to Religion and Politics: Theory and Practice* (London: Routledge, 2013), p. 1.
5   Ibid., p. 2.

dominance shaped the Irish State until, from the 1990s on, it experienced a devastating *dégringolade*. And then, of course, there are the toxic effects of religion on communal relations in Northern Ireland.

All that said, we can't, and shouldn't, keep religion out of politics or world affairs, insisted former US secretary of state Madeleine Albright. 'As I travel around the world,' she wrote in a 2007 book:

> I am often asked, 'Why can't we just keep religion out of foreign policy?' My answer is that we can't and shouldn't. Religion is a large part of what motivates people and shapes their views of justice and right behaviour. It must be taken into account. Nor can we expect our leaders to make decisions in isolation from their religious beliefs. There is a limit to how much the human mind can compartmentalise. In any case, why should world leaders who are religious act and speak as if they are not. We must live with our beliefs and also with our differences; it does no good to deny them.[6]

In the course of history, the three great monotheistic religions – Judaism, Christianity and Islam – have all been used to confer legitimacy on secular regimes.

> Religion has always been linked to legitimacy. In fact, for much of Western history religious legitimacy was a prerequisite to rule. Until the past few centuries, in the West the Church was a central basis for legitimating the government. It was believed that the king ruled through divine right. This 'descending' theory of political legitimacy has it that power descends from God and is granted to the king. This is why the clergy played a central role in coronation ceremonies. By placing the crown on the king's head, they were stating that the king's right to rule came from God. Under such a theory of legitimacy, people have no right to oppose their rulers, because to do so is to oppose God.[7]

---

6   Madeleine Albright, *The Mighty and the Almighty: Reflections on America, God, and World Affairs* (London: Pan Books, 2007), p. 283.

7   Fox, *An Introduction to Religion and Politics*, p. 74.

Today, while the divine right to rule has been abandoned throughout Western societies, it endures in the Islamic world. However, even in the West the notion of a God-given right to rule lingers in however etiolated a form, especially among monarchical families. In the hugely popular Netflix series *The Crown*, for instance, there is a scene in Buckingham Palace where it is explained to the young Queen Elizabeth II (played by Claire Foy) that she rules by divine right. 'That's why the monarch is anointed in a cathedral and why an archbishop, not a politician, places the crown on the monarch's head.' Claiming a divine mandate obviously enhances one's legitimacy in the eyes of the citizenry; that, at any rate, is the theory. The doctrine asserts that a monarch is subject to no earthly authority (such as parliament), deriving his or her right to rule directly from the will of God. The mandate comes from heaven. In this context, we shouldn't forget that the absolute monarchy that is the papacy embraces this doctrine, and is founded upon it.

Much nearer to home, the quest for legitimacy both internally and on the international stage was a significant preoccupation of the newly independent Irish State, which had come into being (provisionally) as a result of the Anglo-Irish Treaty of December 1921. The government of the Irish Free State – which had survived a challenge in arms to its legitimacy (the Civil War of 1922–3) – was keen to establish a stronger international profile. In mid-1928 steps were taken to establish a consulate in Berlin and Paris. But a desire to establish diplomatic relations with the Holy See was a central concern. Dr Dermot Keogh, professor emeritus of Irish history at UCC, explained why:

> The Irish Free State was known to have wanted to exchange envoys with the Holy See for a number of years. Firstly, Rome had a prestige which neither Berlin nor Paris enjoyed in the country. Secondly, a nuncio in Dublin would enhance the standing of the government and lend greater legitimacy to the Free State. Thirdly, the presence of a nuncio in Dublin could help give the government more control over the bishops. Fourthly, an Irish envoy resident in Rome would allow the Irish government to represent itself efficiently at the Vatican. That, in turn, would help counter the

anti-Cumann na nGaedheal bias of the Irish College. The benefits were so obvious that the government could have been faulted for not doing so sooner.[8]

Diplomatic relations would be established in 1929 when Paschal Robinson was named apostolic nuncio to Ireland. It marked the beginning of what Professor Keogh has called the 'special relationship' between Ireland and the Holy See.[9]

---

8   Dermot Keogh, *Ireland and the Vatican: The Politics and Diplomacy of Church–State Relations, 1922–1960* (Cork: Cork University Press, 1995), pp. 36–7.

9   Ibid., p. 30.

Chapter 3

GOD'S TERRORISTS

Theology is politically important,
and those who engage in either
theology or politics ignore this
fact at a certain peril.

William T. Cavanaugh

Political religion might be said to be the public expression – the acting out in the public square – of an underlying political theology. And the latter is formed and formulated on the basis of the conviction that belief in a deity ultimately has political implications and political consequences. This is certainly true of the three great monotheistic faiths – Judaism, Christianity and Islam.

In her excellent book *Political Theology*, Elizabeth Phillips acknowledges 'the claim that when religion goes public, when theology gets mixed up with politics, things go terribly wrong. Look at Christian fundamentalists bombing abortion clinics in America, some will say. Look at the history of strife in Northern Ireland. Look at the interminable conflict in Israel/ Palestine. Look at George W. Bush and Tony Blair leading the West into war in the Middle East.'

This, she concedes, will lead some people to exclaim that the last thing we need is more political theology.

And yet theological claims and motivations crop up again and again in political discourse and in the political realities of our lives. Whether we are talking about going to war or the regulation of biological and genetic sciences or what government should be doing in times of financial crisis, the theological is there. It is there in overt ways, such as the 'God bless America' and 'punish the evildoers' rhetoric in the United States or the Archbishop of Canterbury's public questioning of the government's budget cuts in the United Kingdom. It is also there in less overt ways whenever we are considering issues which involve the meaning and purpose of human life and human sociality, and how we order our lives together.[1]

In an Irish context, we witnessed the intrusion of theology and religion in a very real way in the campaign leading to the referendum to repeal the Eighth Amendment to the Constitution in May 2018. And we saw it again more recently with the decision by a group of five public figures, including two TDs and a senator, to take a case to the European Court of Human Rights seeking a ruling that the compulsory recitation of a religious oath in public by the president and judges on taking office is discriminatory.[2]

As for a working definition of 'political theology' and, by extension, 'political religion', it is hard to improve on the definition used by William T. Cavanaugh and Peter Scott:

> Theology is broadly understood as discourse about God, and human persons as they relate to God. The political is broadly understood as the use of structural power to organise a society or community of people ... Political theology is, then, the analysis and criticism of political arrangements (including cultural-psychological, social and economic aspects) from the perspective of differing interpretations of God's ways with the world.[3]

---

1   Elizabeth Phillips, *Political Theology* (London: T&T Clark International, 2012), p. 2.

2   *The Irish Times*, 3 August 2021.

3   Peter Scott and William T. Cavanaugh, eds, *The Blackwell Companion to Political Theology* (Oxford: Blackwell, 2004), p. 2.

There have always been links between religion and politics. The latest and most dramatic and traumatic reminder of this was the victory of the Taliban in Afghanistan in August 2021, and the establishment there of an Islamic Emirate.

Commenting on this in an editorial, the *Guardian* said: 'A Western-made "liberal democracy" has fallen into the hands of religious fanatics linked to al-Qaida.'[4] As for the consequences of the Taliban triumph after a twenty-year war, alarm bells were soon sounding both within Afghanistan itself (what now of women's rights after the imposition of Islamic law?) and much further afield.

Polly Toynbee was in no doubt about the 'bitter lesson' as the Taliban turned the clock back twenty years. 'Here ends the West's grotesque delusion that it could use its military might to turn Afghanistan into a stable democracy and a shining path of moderate Islam.'[5]

Far from 'moderate' Islam, the Taliban are imposing an extremist brand of Islam, with dire consequences for women. Recalling her own earlier visit to Afghanistan, Toynbee recalled what she had experienced. 'The Taliban and its pathological loathing of women didn't spring from nowhere – the patriarchal structure of Afghanistan was clear. Women were still shrouded in burqas with vision-blocking grilles.'[6] And one of the early reports after the fall of Kabul noted that some women were searching desperately for burqas.

The best background to the rise of militant Islam is found in Jason Burke's book *Al-Qaeda: The True Story of Radical Islam*. Burke, now the prize-winning Africa correspondent for the *Guardian*, highlighted the emphasis placed by the Deobandis on a rigid observance of a literal reading of Qur'anic injunctions. He added that the Deobandis venerate the ulema (the body of Islamic scholars) and recognise the authority of the clergy and their monopoly on the textual interpretation. It is the Deobandis from whom the Taliban evolved. What we are talking about here is a theocracy in its purest form.

---

4 *The Guardian*, 17 August 2021.

5 *Irish Examiner*, 18 August 2021.

6 Ibid.

Burke explains that the Deobandi movement began in India in the nineteenth century 'in reaction to the challenge posed by British power and Hindu demographic superiority to Indian Muslims. In this they follow the path of revivalist and reformist movements within Islam reacting to external threats'. Part of this reaction was a reorganisation and expansion of madrassas (religious schools or colleges).

> The madrassas, and the ulema who taught in them and were charged with interpreting the external world by the texts, thus became the central focus of the Deobandi movement ... The students at the madrassas were known as *taliban*, a Persianised plural of an Arabic word meaning seekers of knowledge or students. It was these same students who were to form the foot soldiers of the eponymous movement in Afghanistan in the mid-1990s.[7]

According to Burke, in 1879 there were twelve Deobandi madrassas – by 1967 there were nine thousand across South Asia, including nearly a thousand in Pakistan.

> Their growth accelerated during the 1980s, and by 1988 nearly 400,000 boys and young men were being educated by Deobandis in Pakistan. The key to the growth was the huge funds that flowed into the Deobandi madrassas from the Gulf where governments and donors there had decided that the Deobandis were the closest local equivalent to the Wahhabis and thus should be sponsored as part of the global push to encourage the spread of hardline Salafi strands of Islam.[8]

Charles Allen concurs: these madrassas 'promoted an uncompromising, puritanical and exclusive fundamentalism no less restrictive than Wahhabism'.[9]

---

7   Jason Burke, *Al-Qaeda: The True Story of Radical Islam* (London: Penguin Books, 2007), p. 93.

8   Ibid.

9   Charles Allen, *God's Terrorists: The Wahhabi Cult and the Hidden Roots of Modern Jihad* (London: Little, Brown, 2006), p. 208.

Writing days after the fall of Kabul, Michael Jansen, an expert on the Middle East and international affairs, warned about believing early Taliban claims that the movement has become more moderate since it imposed repressive theocratic rule in 1996–2001, when medieval social and cultural structures were imposed and torture and executions were widespread.

> Although the Taliban have declared they will not allow jihadis to mount attacks outside the country, a number of groups, including al-Qaeda, continue to operate in Afghanistan, which could act as a magnet for multiple radical factions seeking indoctrination and training.
>
> The Taliban have made it clear they are committed to the rule of Sharia, rather than democracy. The movement's ideology has been drawn from the theology of India's nineteenth-century revivalist religious-nationalist Sunni Deobandi movement, which adopt hardline Saudi Wahhabism.[10]

Meanwhile two things came into sharp focus: (1) the success of the Taliban would not have been possible without backing from Pakistan, and (2) the return of the Taliban will be a boon for international jihadism. As Lydia Khalil, an expert on international terrorism at the Lowly Institute in Sydney, has emphasised, the Taliban and al-Qaeda 'are deeply aligned with ideology and a vision of Islamic governance'.

All of this is the story of religious radicalisation and the re-emergence of radical Islam in Asia, with unforeseeable geopolitical repercussions. The victory of the Taliban presages a repressive, misogynistic theocratic regime, exhibiting the deeply toxic side of religion. But that's by no means the full story.

---

10   *The Irish Times*, 21 August 2021.

Chapter 4

LIBERATION THEOLOGY

There is no such thing as
private Christian faith.

Giles Fraser

In 1970, when Mary Kenny was woman's editor of the *Irish Press* where I was religious affairs correspondent, she came to me as Holy Week was approaching and suggested that I do an article about the events of Holy Thursday and Good Friday. But do it, she said, in the form of a news report as though I were a reporter in Jerusalem at the time.

The idea appealed to me and I presented Jesus (in two articles) as a revolutionary figure, regarded by the Jewish establishment and the occupying Roman authorities as a dangerous subversive who posed a threat to the established order and the security of the State. The stance he was taking had very clear political implications. He was on the side of the poor, the outcast and the marginalised, and was preaching the need for a just society. Jesus was exercising his ministry in a way that was clearly political: that was the perception and this was why he and his followers came to be regarded as 'enemies of the State'.

Jesus was regarded as a rabble-rouser, a political agitator, a troublemaker, and had to be silenced. The implications of his message were spelled out for the Roman representative in Jerusalem, Pontius Pilate, the Procurator of Judea, by the Sanhedrin (supreme religious and judicial council of the Jews), leaving Pilate with little or no room for manoeuvre, so Jesus's fate after his arrest in the Garden of Gethsemane was predetermined. Just politics, you see.

Mary liked the articles and they were generally well received; I can't recall any negative reaction to them, not even from clerical circles (remember, John Charles McQuaid was still the archbishop of Dublin at the time). Portraying Jesus as a Che Guevara-type figure wasn't nearly as fanciful as some would claim. A society in which liberty, brotherhood, equality and egalitarian structures might become the norm isn't something that the Sermon on the Mount is hostile to; the Kingdom of God could be realised on earth.

In October 1971 I was in Rome for the Synod of Bishops which declared 'the proclamation of justice' to be 'a constituent part of the preaching of the gospel'. Earlier that year, on 14 May, Pope Paul VI published *Octogesima adveniens,* an apostolic letter marking the eightieth anniversary of *Rerum novarum* by Leo XIII, the first of the great social encyclicals and one that came to be known as 'The Workers' Charter'.

In this letter Pope Paul said: 'The Christian has the duty to take part in the organisation and life of political society.' This happens in a variety of ways in different social settings. In Latin America in the 1960s it was to take on a specific and, some would say, very radical form. The circumstances that contributed to this would provide – perhaps 'provoke' is a better word – a new way of looking at religion and its relationship to and role in society.

In 1968 I had been sent by my editor Tim Pat Coogan to Bogota, the capital of Colombia, to cover the visit there of Paul VI. In the course of that visit the Pope travelled to Medellín, a city about an hour's flying time northwest of the capital. He went there because the city was hosting a meeting of CELAM (the Conference of Latin American Bishops). The Latin American bishops, in what one commentator described as 'their epoch-making meeting', made an explicit commitment to take 'a preferential option for the poor'. That meeting provided a foundation for 'liberation theology', though that term wasn't used until later.

In Bogota I was to experience first-hand the conditions which gave rise to this – the distressing reality of the dehumanisation of people through economic exploitation and political repression, and glaring inequalities of wealth on a scale I had never witnessed before.

After a tour of the barrios, the shanty towns on the outskirts of Bogota where the poorest of the poor lived in tin huts, the late Cardinal William Conway, who was representing the Irish hierarchy, appeared shocked, and said to me in an off-the-record comment during an interview that if he lived in Colombia he could understand why people 'would turn to the gun'. At the time the name of Camilo Torres, a priest who joined the National Liberation Army (ELN) and who was killed in February 1966 when the ELN ambushed a Colombian army patrol, was revered in certain sections of society, especially by politically active young people. Torres, who was thirty-seven when he was killed, famously said: 'If Jesus were alive today, he would be a guerrilla'. He had worked during his life (he lectured in sociology at the National University of Colombia) to reconcile Marxism with Catholicism.

It would be another three years before Gustavo Gutiérrez, professor of theology at the Catholic University in Lima, Peru, would publish his landmark book *A Theology of Liberation*. It would appear first in a Spanish edition in 1971, after Gutiérrez had served as an adviser to the Medellín Conference. This is the opening paragraph of the introduction to the original edition:

> This book is an attempt at reflection, based on the gospel and the experiences of men and women committed to the process of liberation in the oppressed and exploited land of Latin America. It is a theological reflection born of the experience of shared efforts to abolish the current unjust situation and to build a different society, freer and more human. Many in Latin America have started along the path of a commitment to liberation, and among them is a growing number of Christians; whatever the validity of these pages, it is due to their experiences and reflections. My greatest desire is not to betray their experiences and efforts to elucidate the meaning of their solidarity with the oppressed.[1]

---

1   Gustavo Gutiérrez, *A Theology of Liberation: History, Politics, and Salvation* (New York: Orbis Books, 1994) (15th anniversary edn), p. xiii.

Later on, in a new introduction to his book, Gutiérrez invoked the influence of Pope John XXIII.

> The expression 'preferential option for the poor' had an important and significant predecessor. I refer to John XXIII's statement, a month before the opening of Vatican II, that the Church is called upon to be a Church of the poor.[2]

Emphasising that the relationship between the gospel and politics was a very old one, Gutiérrez said it was also very contemporary and had taken on a new dimension which had brought a fundamental question to the fore: 'What is the *meaning of the faith* in a life committed to the struggle against injustice and alienation?'[3]

Gutiérrez was seeking to connect and apply the gospel to a world scarred by the starvation of millions, the humiliation of races regarded as inferior, discrimination against women, systematic social injustice, and the persistent violation of human rights.

In the preface to the *Cambridge Companion to Liberation Theology*, Christopher Rowland, professor of the exegesis of holy scripture at the University of Oxford, wrote:

> Liberation theology is not only of interest to theologians but also to all those studying the role of religion in contemporary society. The emphasis on the political dimension of the Church's mission within situations of extreme poverty has made it the most compelling example of political theology in the late twentieth century.[4]

It raises in a very specific, direct and challenging way the following question: 'Does the New Testament have socio-political implications?' And it answers that question very definitely in the affirmative.

---

2   Ibid., p. xxvi.

3   Ibid., p. 74.

4   Christopher Rowland, ed., *The Cambridge Companion to Liberation Theology* (Cambridge: Cambridge University Press, 1999), p. xiii.

Karol Wojtyła from Poland (John Paul II), who was Paul's successor in 1978 (his immediate successor, Albino Luciani [John Paul I] had died suddenly after just thirty-three days in office) was suspicious of liberation theology from the outset, and, in 1979, he made this known. Peter Hebblethwaite wrote:

> Just when liberation theology seemed poised for its greatest expansion, a pope appeared who was hostile to it. As a Pole, Pope John Paul II had seen the bankruptcy of Marxism and could not understand why Christians should feel they had anything to learn from it. The Latin American enthusiasm for borrowing some Marxist concepts seemed like the height of naiveté. At the first available opportunity, namely his visit to the CELAM conference in Puebla, Mexico, in 1979, he declared roundly that 'the idea of Christ as a political figure, a revolutionary, as a subversive man from Nazareth, does not tally with the Church's catechesis'. He also said it was wrong to identify the Kingdom of God with a political realm, and scotched the notion that Catholic social doctrine was out of date.[5]

Later the Pope's reservations and objections would be amplified in a document from the Congregation for the Doctrine of the Faith (CDF) – the Vatican department charged with enforcing orthodoxy in Church teaching – which was headed at the time by Cardinal Joseph Ratzinger (who would succeed Wojtyła, becoming Pope Benedict XVI in 2005).

Those who thought that the Wojtyła–Ratzinger alliance against liberation theology would spell its demise would be disappointed, even though harsh measures were taken by the Vatican against some of its leading proponents.

'Liberation theology is in a less friendly theological and ecclesial climate,' Peter Hebblethwaite conceded in a 1999 essay.

> Indeed, the Prefect for the Congregation for the Doctrine of the Faith, Cardinal Joseph Ratzinger, seems to believe that he has put a stop to liberation theologians' attempts 'to turn religion …

---

5   Ibid., p. 182.

into the handmaiden of political ideologies'. But reports of liberation theology's demise have been exaggerated. Even if bishops sympathetic to liberation theology may be less numerous than they once were, and the particular theological ethos in the immediate aftermath of the Second Vatican Council less apparent, the influence of the liberation theologians on the theological positions of the Roman Catholic Church is everywhere apparent in its official statements.

However vociferous the critics of liberation theology may have become, the pressing needs of the majority of men, women and children in our world only add force to the challenge to Catholic theology from Jon Sobrino: 'If those doing liberation theology are not doing it well, let others do it and do it better.'[6]

Since the election of Jorge Mario Bergoglio of Argentina as Pope Francis in 2013, the climate where liberation theology is concerned has become much more friendly. Gutiérrez has been to Rome at the invitation of the Pope, and, much more significantly, Francis canonised the martyred Archbishop Óscar Romero in October 2018, having beatified him in 2015. For years the campaign to bring this about was blocked in the Vatican during the Wojtyła-Ratzinger pontificates.

Perhaps if Karl Marx had witnessed liberation theology he might not have been so harshly critical of religion, though, as Malory Nye has pointed out, it wasn't religion *per se* that angered Marx, rather it was the way it had come to be used, thus becoming the 'opium of the people'. Russell T. McCutcheon described it thus:

Karl Marx (1818–1883), whose work in political economy understood religion to be a pacifier that both deadened oppressed people's sense of pain and alienation while, simultaneously, preventing them from doing something about their lot in life, since ultimate responsibility was thought to reside with a being who existed outside history.[7]

---

6   Ibid., pp. 196–7.

7   Christopher Partridge, ed., *Introduction to World Religions* (Oxford: Lion, 2005), p. 12.

Nye has put it like this:

> Marx saw religion as having a particular role within the processes
> of oppression and exploitation. He argued that religion (and here
> he had in mind particularly Christianity and Judaism) was not in
> itself a bad thing, but that it helped to facilitate the processes of
> exploitation. It did this through masking the harsh economic and
> political realities of life with a warmer, more comfortable glow.
> If it were not for religion, the working classes would see their
> exploitation more clearly. As such, the ideology of religion is a
> false consciousness, representing reality in a distorted way. And
> because so many religions tend to present the world in which
> existing social relations are not only 'natural' but also 'god-given'
> (or divinely ordained), religion does the dirty work of keeping the
> oppressed content with their oppression.[8]

An older generation of Irish people will be very familiar with the notion that
you put up with life, however harsh, in this 'vale of tears' in the belief that, if
you remained true to the Catholic Church and did what its leaders expected
of you – 'pray, pay and obey' – you would be rewarded in the next life.

In the nineteenth century Marx was dismissive of this when he sat
down with Engels to write *The Communist Manifesto*, and in the twentieth
century so were the creators of liberation theology. The pioneers of
liberation theology sought to use religion as a revolutionary tool. They
didn't regard faith as something passive. The latter (religious faith) when
acted upon – when praxis follows on from belief and reflection on that
belief so that its socio-political implications are grasped – becomes, in
effect, political religion. By 'praxis' here, I mean 'action oriented towards
changing society', in the words of Gramsci. This has been heroically
exemplified by the ministry and witness of those such as Archbishop
Hélder Câmara in Brazil and Archbishop Óscar Romero in El Salvador,
among many others. In Romero's case bearing witness to the gospel cost
him his life.

---

8   Nye, *Religion*, pp. 58–9.

One of the central attractions of political religion is its presentation of religion not as a source of solace and consolation, but as a transformative agency animated by the conviction that the call of Christ is to end injustice now, to liberate humans from oppression now, and to seek the Kingdom of God in this world, not console ourselves by anticipating it in the next.

It was in part the reaction to this false dualism that produced liberation theology, though the Second Vatican Council (1962–5) provided a launching pad (as Hebblethwaite pointed out in his biography of Pope Paul VI) in one of its key documents. In chapter IV of this document (*Pastoral Constitution on the Church in the Modern World*) we find these passages:

> It is a mistake to think that, because we have here no lasting city, but seek the city which is to come, we are entitled to evade our earthly responsibilities ... One of the gravest errors of our time is the dichotomy between the faith which many profess and their day-to-day conduct ... Christians who shirk their temporal duties shirk their duties towards his neighbour, neglect God himself, and endanger their eternal salvation.[9]

But those who speak out in defence of the poor or seek socio-economic reform in their pursuit of justice often place themselves in mortal peril, as we saw in the case of Óscar Romero. Noam Chomsky leaves readers in no doubt that 'political religion' came to be viewed by administrations in Washington DC (notably the Kennedy, Johnson, Nixon and Reagan governments) as a very real threat to American interests in Latin America where brutal dictatorships were the order of the day, and where their armies were trained, financed and backed by Washington.

> The US wars in Latin America from 1960 to 1990, quite apart from their horrors, have long-term historical significance. To consider just one important aspect, they were in no small measure wars against the Catholic Church, undertaken to crush a terrible heresy proclaimed at Vatican II in 1962. At that time, Pope John XXIII 'ushered in a new era

---

9   Austin Flannery, ed., *Vatican Council II: The Basic Sixteen Documents* (Dublin: Dominican Publications, 1996), p. 211.

in the history of the Catholic Church,' in the words of the distinguished theologian Hans Kung, restoring the teachings of the gospels that had been put to rest in the fourth century when the Emperor Constantine established Christianity as the religion of the Roman Empire, thereby instituting 'a revolution' that converted 'the persecuted Church' to a 'persecuting Church'. The heresy of Vatican II was taken up by Latin American bishops, who adopted the 'preferential option of the poor'. Priests, nuns, and laypersons then brought the radical pacifist message of the gospels to the poor, helping them organise to ameliorate their bitter fate in the domains of US power.[10]

Those who called for freedom and justice in Latin America were often the targets of assassination squads. 'In the 1980s, the US, under Ronald Reagan, ravaged Central America in proxy wars to forestall or topple leftist governments,' according to Jeffrey D. Sachs, university professor at Colombia University.[11] Supporters of such 'leftist' governments – often priests and nuns, but also social workers, teachers and trade unionists – were fair game for US-backed death squads who assumed they were Communist extremists. State terror was directed at manifestations of 'political religion' seeking to defend and uphold human rights and human dignity and campaigning against the exploitation and plundering of the poor.

On 24 March 1980, Archbishop Óscar Romero was shot dead by a paid assassin while saying Mass in El Salvador's capital, San Salvador. Over the previous three years he had spoken out against torture and assassinations by death squads, and vigorously defended human rights.

In *The Joy of the Gospel*, his 2013 apostolic exhortation on the proclamation of the gospel in today's world, Pope Francis was adamant about the socio-political implications of religion: 'It is no longer possible to claim that religion should be restricted to the private sphere and that it exists only to prepare souls for heaven.' On the contrary, he stated that 'all Christians, their pastors included, are called to show concern for the building of a better world'.

---

10   Noam Chomsky, *Who Rules the World?* (London: Penguin Books, 2017), pp. 12–13.
11   *Irish Examiner*, 19 August 2021.

The earth is our common home and all of us are brothers and sisters. If indeed 'the just ordering of society and of the State is a central responsibility of politics', the Church 'cannot and must not remain on the sidelines in the fight for justice'.

In his exhortation he argued 'no one can demand that religion should be relegated to the inner sanctum of personal life, without influence on societal and national life, without concern for the soundness of civil institutions, without a right to offer an opinion on events affecting society … An authentic faith – which is never comfortable or completely personal – always involves a deep desire to change the world, to transmit values, to leave this earth somehow better than we found it.'

On 14 October 2018 Pope Francis canonised Óscar Romero in Rome, in a ceremony that many saw as an endorsement of liberation theology. Under John Paul II and Benedict XVI, Romero's canonisation kept getting delayed, due in the main to concern at high levels in the Vatican not just about Romero himself but about liberation theology and the extent to which he had embraced it.

'Untangling this relationship tells us much about the new saint and how his canonisation represents a de facto landmark recognition of liberation theology as an important way for modern believers to live a faith that addresses the social crises of our times,' wrote Michael E. Lee, associate professor of theology at Fordham University, New York, on the eve of the canonisation.[12]

---

12   *The Tablet*, 13 October 2018.

Chapter 5

NATIONALISM AND RELIGION

If someone suggests there
is no connection between religion and
politics, then they must be
reading a different Bible to my own.

Archbishop Desmond Tutu

The bitter divisions, the bloody conflict, the sectarianism, bigotry and pervasive mistrust that have been so much a part of the fabric of Northern Ireland since Partition, were fuelled to a significant degree by a phenomenon we have come to a new appreciation of in the post-9/11 age – political religion.

This might be best defined as the harnessing and exploitation of religion for political ends – the hijacking of religion to serve secular objectives and goals. There may also, of course, be a reverse dimension – circumstances where you have religion or a church embracing or endorsing or aligning itself with a particular political system or political establishment to advance its own aims. The Catholic Church's alliance with the Irish Free State is an obvious example.

In her book, *Irish Catholicism Since 1950*, Louise Fuller of the Department of History, NUI Maynooth, focuses on this.

One of the outstanding features of Irish Catholic culture in the post-independence era was the extent to which the State, by the actions, words and public appearances of its representatives, legitimated the Catholic ethos. An alliance was formed between the Catholic Church authorities and the Free State government during the Civil War years, and WT Cosgrave during his tenure of office looked to the Church to augment the authority of his government. The alliance was a mutually reinforcing one. The bishops were prepared to throw their weight behind the new State and endorse its political legitimacy which was being contested by the anti-treaty Republicans, and the rulers of the new State were not disposed to question the authority of the Church in matters having to do with education, health or sexual morality, traditionally seen by the Church as its areas of competence.[1]

In its crudest form – and one of its deadliest – political religion in Ireland was best exemplified by the Rev. Ian Paisley and Paisleyism, especially during the period between the publication of the first edition of the scurrilous *Protestant Telegraph* in April 1966 and the Good Friday Agreement of April 1998. But it also had its 'green' variety, as Martin Dillon, a BBC reporter who covered Northern Ireland for eighteen years, has reminded us. 'Catholicism, nationalism and republicanism are interconnected … The folk tradition of the gun in both communities, carries with it a moral crusade in defence of the respective traditions,' he wrote in 1991.[2]

Throughout the nineteenth century, in the long struggle for independence from British rule, it was Catholic nationalism that sustained and legitimised the campaigns for Catholic Emancipation, land reform and Home Rule. Outside of Ireland, there were other, later examples of religion being co-opted on the side of nationalist causes.

'The success of religious nationalism since the latter part of the twentieth century has surprised many commentators who believed that religion no longer had political significance in an era of nation states,' according to Linda Woodhead, professor of sociology of religion at Lancaster University.

1   Louise Fuller, *Irish Catholicism Since 1950: The Undoing of a Culture* (Dublin: Gill and Macmillan, 2004), p. 3.

2   Martin Dillon, *God and the Gun: The Church and Irish Terrorism* (New York: Routledge, 1999), p. 2.

'In 1979, for example, the increasingly secular state in Iran was overthrown by Islamic nationalists. Religious nationalism is also a potent force in many other Islamic countries, as well as in India (Hinduism), Israel (Orthodox Judaism) and the former Yugoslavia (Roman Catholic Christianity, Orthodox Christianity, Islam),' she wrote.[3]

But it wasn't until the twenty-first century that we witnessed the emergence of a political religion with a transnational agenda. This is radical Islam, seeking the establishment of a universal caliphate. Political religion has a very long history, but in its twenty-first-century manifestations it has assumed a very virulent form, characterised by intolerance, misogyny and oppressiveness that blossomed into a hatred of those who profess a different faith. The latter are often categorised and ostracised (or worse) as heretics or infidels or blasphemers. The 'return' of the deity on the global stage (it would be a mistake to assume that the growing disenchantment with and disengagement from institutional religion in Ireland necessarily signifies a loss of faith in God) has been accompanied by a protean phenomenon with a very dark side – the rise and rise of political religion. On 9/11 that dark side showed itself with fearful consequences.

The title of the 2009 book by the editor of the *Economist*, John Micklethwait, and its Washington bureau chief, Adrian Wooldridge – *God is Back* – captured an important if unexpected truth about Western society. It was unexpected because God's obituary, famously penned by the German philosopher Friedrich Nietzsche in 1882 when he declared 'God is dead', had come to be regarded as a defining characteristic of Western culture, especially in the aftermath of two devastating world wars.

Nietzsche had used the phrase to give expression to the notion that the eighteenth-century Enlightenment had 'killed' the possibility of belief in God; he sought to encapsulate the consequences of the Enlightenment for the centrality of the concept of God and belief in God within Western European civilisation, which had been essentially Christian in character since the time of Emperor Constantine.

'Ever since the Enlightenment there has been a schism in Western thought over the relationship between religion and modernity,' Micklethwait and

---

3   Linda Woodhead, ed., *Religions in the Modern World: Traditions and Transformations* (London and New York: Routledge, 2009) (2nd edn), p. 4.

Wooldridge point out in *God is Back*. 'Europeans, on the whole, have assumed that modernity would marginalise religion. Americans, in the main, have assumed that the two things can thrive together ... For most of the past two hundred years the European view of modernity has been in the ascendant.'[4]

They go on to tell us that 'everyone who was anyone in European public life agreed that religion was dying – and that its effect on politics was ebbing'. The European idea, they say, that you cannot become modern without throwing off religion's yoke, had a massive influence all around the world. 'Most trend-setting books in the 1990s saw the world through secular lenses.'[5]

The big game changer was 9/11. Images of the shocking attacks by planes hijacked by nineteen young Muslims on the World Trade Center in New York and the Pentagon in Washington DC will live forever in the memory of all those who witnessed them on television. Viewers could hardly believe what they were seeing.

The geopolitical consequences of those attacks have been immense and far-reaching. The earth may not have stood still on 9/11, but the terrible events of that day dramatically altered the way we look at the world today, at global affairs, and at religion in particular. There is now a very changed appreciation of religion and its role in world affairs.

As has already been highlighted, the 'politicisation' of religion is almost as old as religion itself. Rulers have always been cognisant of the importance of having religion on their side, not because of any innate regard for religion (at least not in all cases) but because of its utility value. A striking example of this was the decision by Napoleon to sign a concordat with Pope Pius VII on 13 July 1801. Napoleon realised that it was better to have the Catholic Church in France on his side. Accordingly, over the centuries secular rulers have plotted and schemed and pursued associations and alliances to gain the advantages and benefits that would accrue from winning over religion.

For secular leaders the primary desire when entering an alliance with a church or a religious organisation is, more often than not, the quest for

---

4   John Micklethwait and Adrian Wooldridge, *God is Back: How the Global Rise of Faith is Changing the World* (London: Penguin Books, 2010), p. 9.

5   Ibid., p. 12.

'legitimacy'. As an example of this pursuit of legitimacy we have already cited the desire of the government of the newly created Irish Free State to establish diplomatic relations with the Vatican. The appointment of a nuncio to Dublin would have enhanced the standing of the government in the eyes of the public and also added a new element of legitimacy to the new State, especially within the international community.

In 1937 this was also a concern of Éamon de Valera when he despatched the Secretary of the Department of External Affairs, Joseph Walshe, on a secret mission to Rome with a draft copy of the new constitution (*Bunreacht na hÉireann*), which was due to be put to the people for ratification by way of a referendum later in the year. De Valera was hoping that Pope Pius XI would endorse the draft, thereby lending it important legitimacy for the voters of Catholic Ireland.

The classic and most potent example of a legitimacy-producing alliance in the twentieth century, and one that would have huge long-term consequences in the twenty-first century, occurred in 1932 and led to the creation of Saudi Arabia. This followed from an historic arrangement between the House of Saud and the House of Al-Wahhab, a firebrand preacher. To secure legitimacy, the House of Saud ceded control of education and justice to the Wahhabi clergy, who implement a fundamentalist form of Islam.

Wahhabism dominates Saudi Arabia (no other religion is tolerated) and supports its ruling dynasty. 'Wahhabism is the form of Islam that is still practised today in Saudi Arabis,' explained Karen Armstrong, 'a puritan religion based on a strict literal interpretation of scripture and early Islamic tradition.'[6]

It is surely one of the great ironies of post-World War II history that the USA made Saudi Arabia a key regional partner in the Middle East, yet it is Saudi Arabia, where the Wahhabi clerical establishment sets the moral agenda, that spent billions of petro-dollars exporting its virulent anti-Western brand of Islam. Fifteen of the nineteen 9/11 hijackers were from Saudi Arabia, as was Osama bin Laden, who masterminded the attacks.

---

6   Karen Armstrong, *Islam: A Short History* (London: Phoenix, 2002), p. 115.

Some terrible things have already happened in this century in God's name, and who is to say that more will not follow? That's the frightening reality of the 'dark side' of political religion in the twentieth century.

It is also true, of course, that history provides us with manifold examples of a fusion of religion and politics that, far from being toxic or sinister, had, and continues to have, a positive, beneficial and enriching effect.

Chapter 6

MURDER IN PARIS

Nothing can be done with a pencil
or a keyboard that warrants
a reprisal with a Kalashnikov.

editorial in the *Economist*

I left Paris on Monday, 5 January 2014 – two days before the murderous attack by Islamist extremists on the offices of the satirical magazine *Charlie Hebdo*, which left twelve people dead. The magazine had published cartoons of the Prophet Muhammad. As the perpetrators ran from the offices to their getaway car, shouts of 'Allahu Akbar' (God is great) were heard. The targeting of *Charlie Hebdo* was followed by the cry 'we have avenged the Prophet Muhammad'.

Earlier that morning, before leaving the French capital, I had spent some time reading *The Case for God: What Religion Really Means* by Karen Armstrong, acquired the day before during my annual pilgrimage to the Shakespeare and Company bookshop, across the Seine from the Notre Dame Cathedral. The book contained this warning about religious fundamentalism: 'In all its forms, fundamentalism is a fiercely reductive faith. In their anxiety and fear, fundamentalists often distort the tradition they are trying to defend.'[1]

---

1   Karen Armstrong, *The Case for God: What Religion Really Means* (New York and London: Vintage Books, 2010), p. 282.

Her words would soon prove prescient: but it is in this very 'distortion' that provides the matrix from which radical Islam springs.

In an editorial after the atrocity in the centre of Paris, the *Guardian* said: 'The hooded thugs trained their Kalashnikovs on free speech everywhere'. What we saw in Paris was an attempt to introduce a blasphemy law through the barrel of a gun. It was an attack on a paper that had become a symbol of free speech in France. The then French president François Hollande said the attack was 'an act of exceptional barbarism'. It was, according to the then UN Secretary-General Ban Ki-moon, 'a direct assault on democracy'.

In an opinion piece in the *Guardian*, Ed Husain, an adjunct senior fellow at the Council on Foreign Relations wrote:

> The murders in Paris are not an isolated incident but part of a global trend of young Muslims disenchanted with the modern world, finding consolation in the theology and ideology of literalist sharia, killing, vengeance, punishment, domination and imposing their worldview as a State law. Al-Qaida, Isis, Somalia's al-Shabaab and others are only manifestations of this mindset. There is a raging battle of ideas within Islam across the world today. The extremism, terrorism and sectarian warfare is an overspill of this intra-faith theological conflict.[2]

Husain had earlier said, 'We cannot let the murderers define Islam'.

Two days after the Husain article, this sentiment was echoed in a letter to the *Irish Times*. 'The killing of journalists in Paris on Wednesday was not an attack on France but also an assault on Islam and the very freedoms that allow thirty million Muslims to prosper in the West. Unfortunately there is a problem of extremism and radicalisation among a minority of Muslim youth in Western countries. It is the responsibility of Muslim leaders to highlight the peaceful and just message of Islam in which there is no space for extremism'. The sender of the letter was Dr Muhammad Umar Al-Qadri of the Al-Mustafa Islamic Educational and Cultural Centre in Dublin.[3]

---

2   *The Guardian*, 8 January 2015.
3   *The Irish Times*, 10 January 2015.

In the aftermath of the massacre at the *Charlie Hebdo* offices, there was an insightful comment from the French actress Juliette Binoche: 'It is terrible and sad to see how manipulative some religious people are – and that is true in any religion – when the real text, the actual religion is not revengeful or hateful; on the contrary, it has a sense of forgiveness and love and care for others,' she said.[4]

Inevitably, perhaps, the murders in Paris – committed by killers who believed they were avenging a previous blasphemy – focused attention on Article 40 of the Constitution of Ireland with its provision against blasphemy. In an *Irish Times* editorial urging repeal, this was described as 'Ireland's antiquated, unworkable and unused blasphemy law'.[5] Five days earlier, the *Irish Examiner*, in an editorial, also backed the need for a referendum on the constitutional ban on blasphemy. It described this as 'a legacy from another time, another place' and said 'its repeal is long overdue'.[6]

If Irish citizens needed a compelling reason why they should vote to remove blasphemy from the Constitution in a referendum that was announced for October 2018, then the case in Pakistan of Asia Bibi, a Christian woman sentenced to death after being convicted of blasphemy against Islam and who had been on death row since 2010 pending an appeal, should have sufficed.

Our then taoiseach Enda Kenny joined other world leaders and thousands of French citizens who assembled in Place de la République in Paris (wherein stands the statue of Marianne, the symbol of the French Republic) on 11 January 2015 in a demonstration of unity against terror after the massacre at the offices of the *Charlie Hebdo* magazine. He was reminded that the Muslim extremists who carried out the attack regarded the magazine's lampooning of the Prophet Muhammad as 'blasphemous'.

Much further back, when Salman Rushdie published his novel *The Satanic Verses* in 1998, it led to what became known as the Rushdie Affair. Many Muslims considered certain passages of the novel to be blasphemous, and in 1989 Ayatollah Khomeini of Iran issued a fatwa ordering Muslims to kill Rushdie. The author had to go into hiding, and the Iranian regime

---

4   Interview with Krissi Murison for the *Sunday Times Magazine*, 25 January 2015.

5   *The Irish Times*, 17 January 2015.

6   *Irish Examiner*, 21 January 2015.

backed the fatwa until 1998 when the government of President Mohammad Khatami said it no longer supported the killing of the novelist.

The Pakistan case was particularly troubling because it concerned a Christian woman who has been on death row since 2010, having been convicted of blasphemy against Islam. The charge against Asia Bibi dates back to a hot day in 2009, when she went to get water for her and her fellow farm workers. Two Muslim women refused to take a drink from a container used by a Christian. A few days later, a mob accused her of blasphemy. She was convicted and sentenced to death.

It had in the past been argued that these matters were far removed from Ireland and that the blasphemy provision here had done no harm. This was to ignore the fact that countries with very strict and even draconian blasphemy laws, such as Pakistan, had not been slow to invoke the example of Ireland in international forums, such as the United Nations, to justify their own measures, often used against members of minority faiths.

The Enda Kenny-led government finally recognised that blasphemy belonged to a bygone age and should not feature in the constitution of a modern, democratic State. Even the Catholic bishops conceded that the provision against blasphemy in the Constitution was 'largely obsolete'. At their autumn conference in Maynooth shortly before the referendum, they acknowledged that the reference to blasphemy in Article 40.6.1 (i) of the Constitution may give rise to concern 'because of the way such measures have been used to justify violence and oppression against minorities in other parts of the world'.[7]

On 1 February 2015, the actor and writer Stephen Fry was Gay Byrne's guest on the RTÉ One series *The Meaning of Life*, and the veteran presenter (who died on 4 November 2019) seemed somewhat taken aback by the robustness with which Fry espoused his own brand of atheism. 'If God created this universe, he's clearly an utter maniac,' declared Fry. The actor's God – if the latter exists at all – is clearly a monster. 'Why should I respect a capricious, mean-minded, stupid God who creates a world which is so

---

7   Irish Catholic Bishop's Conference, 'Submission to the Convention on the Constitution for its consideration on the removal of blasphemy', *Irish Catholic Bishops' Conference*, 4 November 2013, https://www.catholicbishops.ie/2013/11/04/submission-convention-constitution-consideration-removal-blasphemy/ (accessed April 2022).

full of injustice and pain?' We don't know if Fry's version of a maniacal God exists, but terrible things continue to be done in his (or her) name – GOD.

As I mentioned earlier, I left Paris just forty-eight hours before the deadly attack on the offices of the *Charlie Hebdo* magazine. François Hollande called the attack a 'terrorist outrage', but one that was carried out by people motivated by extremist religious beliefs.

The irony – one of several – is that the night before I left my hotel in Paris, I had watched a TV debate on the threat posed by the rise of religious extremism. This followed news coverage of an anti-Islam march in the German city of Dresden. Some eighteen thousand marched through Dresden, with similar but smaller demonstrations in Berlin and Cologne. These marches were coordinated by a far-right organisation called Pegida (Patriotic Europeans Against Islamisation).

What was becoming clear then was that a very dangerous situation was developing – one that posed a threat to society throughout the West. And religion – specifically Islam (or a radical and perverse interpretation of it) – was at the root of this threat.

No religion has a right to claim privileged status, though, of course, for centuries that is precisely what Christianity had in the West. In order to safeguard its privileged status it embarked on bloody crusades against external enemies – Muslims – and instituted a murderous inquisition against internal enemies – heretics.

Christianity learned to adapt – though a residue of its previous claims of privileged status remained in the retention in many legal systems, including our own of the offence of blasphemy.

This is the offence – the mocking of the Prophet Muhammad – for which the staff of *Charlie Hebdo* paid an appalling price. To hold, as some Muslims do, that nothing critical of Muhammad can be spoken or written is to hold a position that directly violates freedom of expression. That was one of the compelling arguments that influenced the Irish people to repeal Article 40.6 of the Constitution of Ireland. On 26 October 2018 in a referendum 64.85 per cent of Irish voters supported the repeal of the blasphemy law.

Chapter 7

GOD AND THE GUN

The history of the tree of religion
with its many branches, as
Mahatma Gandhi would describe the
world's religions, has been long and varied.

Elizabeth Ramsey

If we want to see what political religion looks like, we need look no further than our own backyard. To observe political religion in action, so to speak, our gaze need not extend beyond these shores. Ireland should certainly be our starting point because political religion not only has a long pedigree here, but it has also in recent times spawned a virulent and murderous strand. What came to be known euphemistically as 'the Troubles' (1969–1998) fed on a bitter, deep-rooted, religion-based sectarianism.

Martin Dillon tells of an encounter in the 1970s with Kenny McClinton, a member of the UDR (Ulster Defence Regiment). The latter admitted that 'he once advocated beheading Catholics and impaling their heads on the railings of Woodvale Park in the Protestant Shankhill area of West Belfast. McClinton told his paramilitary boss that he was "up for it" and that it was the best means of terrorising the IRA'.[1]

---

1   Martin Dillon, *God and the Gun: The Church and Irish Terrorism* (New York: Routledge, 1999), p. 19.

Fast-forward to 2014, and with the emergence of the extremist Islamist group Isis we had the gruesome beheadings on video of two American journalists and a British aid worker. These were staged executions with twin aims: publicity for the group and the engendering of terror.

In August 2014 the heading over the editorial in the *Irish Times* was 'Persecuted Christians'. It pointed out that 'the history and destiny of the long-established Christian communities across the Middle East was bound up with the countries where they live', but 'the gains of the Arab Spring have been reversed and Christians now find themselves on the wrong side of the new politics, suffering severe persecution'. The paper reminded its readers that Iraq's three main Christian traditions – Chaldean, Assyrian and Orthodox – dated from the times of the Apostolic Church. The editorial closed with this warning: 'The end of Christianity in the region would impoverish the Middle East and the world politically, socially and culturally'.[2]

The Irish Sun followed with an editorial two days later, which began: 'Anyone who kills in the name of God should go to hell'. This then followed: 'The atrocities being carried out by Isis in Iraq are a stain on humanity. Summary executions, beheadings, crucifixions and now, according to the latest horrific reports, the burying alive of women and children.'[3]

Since those editorials were written there has been a growing appreciation in the West of the threat posed by religious extremism, especially the threat from Islamist fanatics.

Is this one of the compelling reasons why there is so much negativity today about religion? Why is it the object of so much criticism, some of which is irrational? Not only is it reviled and ridiculed in some quarters, it is also being blamed as the source of a whole range of social ills and problems, even to the extent of being cited as the fount of all violence. Some would have us believe that religion is a poisonous flower whose noxious odours infect its adherents with a disposition towards hatred and violence. Karen Armstrong summed up the situation: 'In the West the idea that religion is inherently violent is now taken for granted and seems self-evident'.[4] How did things come to this?

---

2   *The Irish Times*, 9 August 2014.

3   *The Irish Sun*, 11 August 2014.

4   Karen Armstrong, *Fields of Blood: Religion and the History of Violence* (London: The Bodley Head, 2014), p. 1.

Since the ill-fated invasion of Iraq in 2003, we in Ireland have looked upon the evolving, chaotic and bloody situation in the Middle East and Africa with a mixture of puzzlement, incredulity and horror. Of course, one must also include Afghanistan and Pakistan, home to the Taliban and where Osama bin Laden sought refuge. In the midst of all of this we were – or thought we were – observers from afar, but all that changed on 26 June 2015 when thirty-eight people were killed by an Islamic extremist in the Tunisian resort of Sousse. Three of those shot were Irish. We were no longer untouched by the murderous ideology of Islamic State (Isis or Isil). At the funeral Mass for two of the victims in Athlone, Fr Liam Devine told the congregation that whereas heretofore the images on our television screens from dusty parts of the Middle East were 'sanitised and sterilised, now the violence is at our own door'.

This was just one of a series of atrocities that have left many people in the West bewildered and, in some cases, even fearful. Confronted by the senselessness and dumb brutality of terrorist violence, they have begun to question the role of religion in the twenty-first century. As the Dalai Lama, the Tibetan Buddhist leader, said during a surprise visit to the Glastonbury Festival in June 2015: 'Humans killing each other in the name of religious faith – unthinkable'. And yet the unthinkable is happening.

What are we to make of this? What is going on? We wanted explanations, we wanted to understand how barbaric acts could be justified in the name of God. Many of us have struggled to comprehend what a front page headline in the *Times* of London in August 2014 called 'Wars of religion'. The story that followed said jihadists in Iraq had forced up to one hundred thousand Christians and other minority faiths to flee. 'Isis, the ultra-violent Islamist group, was reported to be carrying out crucifixions and beheadings as it surged forward to carve out a Muslims-only caliphate in northern Iraq and Syria.'[5]

An editorial inside, also headed 'Wars of religion', said Isis was laying claim to being an even more fearsome terrorist franchise than al-Qaeda. 'It commands little more than seven thousand active fighters, yet it is paralysing international action, ruthlessly beheading Shia believers, chasing Christians

---

5   *The Times*, 8 August 2014.

out of their communities, battling the Kurds and now directly threatening the Yazidis.' The editorial went on to explain that neither Muslims nor Christians, the Yazidis – Iraq's most ancient sect – were closest to the Zoroastrian faith, and were viewed by the jihadists as 'devil-worshippers'.[6]

What were readers in the West to make of this? The Shias represent one great branch of Islam, but they are also being targeted by Isis. Its members are Sunnis, the other great branch of Islam, though they subscribe to a very strict and fundamentalist version of Sunni Islam known as Wahhabism. The division between Shias and Sunnis has very old roots – it goes all the way to the seventh century and stems from a dispute over who should succeed the Prophet Muhammad.

---

6   *The Times*, 8 August 2014.

Chapter 8

RELIGIOUS RIVALRIES

Students of history recognise all too well
the dangers posed by political leaders
who see themselves as God's surrogates.

Madeleine Albright

In 2006 Madeleine Albright, who served as US secretary of state from 1997 to 2001, the first woman ever to hold the position, published a book that was described in the blurb as 'a provocative look at the role of religion in world affairs'.[1] The book's subtitle was 'Reflections on America, God, and World Affairs'.

Albright, who had been appointed by President Bill Clinton, left office in January 2001 after the inauguration of George W. Bush as the forty-third president. This was eight months before the dreadful events of 9/11, events which compelled a major rethink about the impact of religion on world affairs.

Prior to 9/11 religion seemed to be on the wane, certainly in the West. Surveying the scene, one would have to conclude that the lines from Matthew Arnold's 1853 poem 'Dover Beach' were prophetic:

---

1   Madeleine Albright, *The Mighty and the Almighty: Reflections on America, God, and World Affairs* (London: Pan Books, 2007).

The sea of faith
Was once, too, at the full, and round earth's shore
Lay like the folds of a bright girdle furl'd;
But now I only hear
Its melancholy, long, withdrawing roar ...

Towards the end of the nineteenth century the German philosopher Friedrich Nietzsche made his famous 'God is dead!' pronouncement (in his 1883 book *Thus Spoke Zarathustra*). In 1996 *Time* magazine published arguably its best cover ever – the Easter issue on 8 April 1966 posed the provocative question in huge red type against a black background: 'Is God Dead?'

Ever since the Enlightenment in the eighteenth century the conviction had grown that religion was on the wane and would, in due course, be displaced by rationalism and science.

> Armed with science, reason, and empirical facts, the Enlightenment saw itself as engaged in a noble struggle against the constricting medieval darkness of Church dogma and popular superstition, tied to a backward and tyrannical political structure of corrupt privilege. The cultural authority of dogmatic religion was recognised as inherently inimical to personal liberty and unhampered intellectual speculation and discovery. By implication, the religious sensibility itself – except in rationalised, deistic form – could well be seen as antagonistic to human freedom.[2]

However, it was really the emergence of secular nation states in the aftermath of the French Revolution in 1789 that posed a direct challenge to religion and Church authority.

'There are few religions which have not been profoundly affected by the rise of the nation state,' according to Linda Woodhead.

> Nations themselves are not new (ancient Israel was a nation, for example), but what is new is the rise of the secular nation state

---

2   Richard Tarnas, *The Passion of the Western Mind: Understanding the Ideas That Have Shaped Our World View* (London: Pimlico, 1991), p. 312.

with its extensive apparatus of control over a huge range of aspects of social and political life. What is also new is the way in which the nation state has become the almost universal unit of territorial control worldwide. Increasingly, such states are constitutional, that is to say they exist to serve not just those who rule but those who are ruled, and their power is checked in order to protect the freedom of their citizens. They are secular in the sense that they seek to keep religion out of politics.[3]

The origins of the modern sovereign state can be traced back to the Treaty of Westphalia of 1648, which ended the Thirty Years' War. However, religion and religious leaders continued to play an influential and, in some cases, dominant role in public affairs. The French Revolution changed that, but the formation of the nation state wouldn't reach its full flowering until the nineteenth century when powerful states like Germany and Italy emerged – states that were combatively secular.

These nation states were 'modern' in that they marked a break with the previous era, and modernity would have a transformative effect. Increasingly, it became equated with secularisation. 'Secularisation, or the decline of religion, has often been seen as an inevitable consequence of modernisation,' noted Linda Woodhead.[4]

The secularisation thesis quickly took hold. 'As Europe's economic and political life developed, religion diminished in public significance; religious aspirations were increasingly relegated to the private sphere,' according to Grace Davie, senior lecturer in sociology at the University of Exeter. 'Secularisation was a necessary part of modernisation, and as the world modernised, it would automatically secularise. But if this was so, how could the very different situation in the United States be explained?' For this was a society marked, unlike Europe, by what Davie called 'the successful cohabitation of vibrant religiosity and developed modernity'.[5] For Davie the answer is clear: the 'secularisation thesis'

---

3   Linda Woodhead, ed., *Religions in the Modern World: Traditions and Transformations* (London and New York: Routledge, 2009) (2nd edn), p. 3.

4   Ibid., p. 8.

5   Grace Davie, 'Europe: The Exception that Proves the Rule?' in Peter L. Berger, ed., *The Desecularization of the World: Resurgent Religion and World Politics* (Grand Rapids: WB Eerdmans Publishing Company, 1999), p. 76.

is disproved by the evidence not just from the United States but elsewhere also. As Madeleine Albright acknowledged in 2009: 'Almost everywhere, religious movements are thriving'.

In the introductory essay to *The Desecularization of the World*, which he edited, Peter L. Berger, one of the world's leading sociologists of religion, challenged this secularisation thesis head-on. 'My point is that the assumption that we live in a secularised world is false. The world today, with some exceptions … is as furiously religious as it ever was, and in some places more so than ever.'[6]

Berger was writing in 1999; then in 2018, this was the opening paragraph in a long article in the *Guardian* by Harriet Sherwood: 'If you think religion belongs to the past and we live in a new age of reason, you need to check out the facts: 84% of the world's population identifies with a religious group. Members of this demographic are generally younger and produce more children than those who have no religious affiliation, so the world is getting more religious, not less – although there are significant geographical variations'.

As to which religions are growing, and where, Sherwood's article said: 'The short answer is religion is on the wane in Western Europe and North America, and it's growing everywhere else … [and] Islam is the fastest-growing religion – more than twice as fast as the overall global population.'[7]

The article also forecast that Christianity was likely to lose its top spot in the world religion league to Islam by the middle of the twenty-first century. 'Had an enterprising fortune-teller predicted four decades ago that in the twenty-first-century religion would become a formidable force in global politics, educated people would have considered him a laughingstock.' So wrote Monica Duffy Toft, Daniel Philpott and Timothy Samuel Shah in 2011.[8]

Madeleine Albright's experience as a diplomat supports this:

> I cannot remember any leading American diplomat speaking in depth about the role of religion in shaping the world. Religion

---

6   Ibid., p. 2.

7   *The Guardian*, 27 August 2018.

8   Monica Duffy Toft, Daniel Philpott and Timothy Samuel Shah, *God's Century* (New York and London: W.W. Norton & Company), 2011, p. 1.

was not a respecter of national borders; it was above and beyond reason; it evoked the deepest passions; and historically, it was the cause of much bloodshed. Diplomats in my era were taught not to invite trouble, and no subject seemed more inherently treacherous than religion.[9]

Pointing out that the wars between Catholics and Protestants that had claimed the lives of one-third of Christian Europe had been brought to a close in 1648 by the Peace of Westphalia, she said she found it 'incredible', as the twenty-first century approached, that Catholics and Protestants were still quarrelling in Northern Ireland and that Hindus and Muslims were still squaring off against each other in South Asia.

> Surely, I thought, these rivalries were the echoes of earlier, less enlightened times, not a sign of battles still to come. Since the terror attacks of 9/11, I have come to realise that it may have been I who was stuck in an earlier time. Like many other foreign policy professionals, I have had to adjust the lens through which I view the world.[10]

This is a world where, as Albright acknowledged, religious movements are thriving almost everywhere. We are left to ponder the implications of this phenomenon.

> How can we best manage events in a world in which there are many religions, with belief systems that flatly contradict one another at key points? How do we deal with the threat posed by extremists who, acting in the name of God, try to impose their will on others? We know that the nature of this test extends back to pagan times and is therefore nothing new; what is new is the extent of damage violence can inflict. This is where technology has truly made a difference. A religious war fought with swords, chain mail, catapults, and battering rams is one thing. A war fought with high

---

9   Albright, *The Mighty and the Almighty*, p. 8.
10   Ibid., p. 9.

explosives against civilian targets is quite another. And the prospect of a nuclear bomb detonated by terrorists in purported service to the Almighty is a nightmare that may one day come true.[11]

Towards the end of her book, Albright (who died on 23 March 2022) offered a defence of 'political religion' on the grounds that people of faith are entitled to have political beliefs, just like other people.

> We had better accept that the world is filled with political Muslims, political Christians, political Jews, and political people of every other faith. It is no crime to have a political agenda. It is a crime, however, to act on a violent and lawless one. That distinction must be clear.[12]

In expressing abhorrence for a brand of 'political Islam' linked to violent jihad and committed to waging a 'holy war', we also, she says, need to be mindful and supportive of another brand of 'political Islam' – one that 'fights for economic opportunity, personal freedom, and peaceful relations within and among the peoples of the world'.[13]

---

11   Ibid., pp. 10–11.

12   Ibid., p. 297.

13   Ibid., p. 298.

Chapter 9

SHADES OF A THEOCRACY

In a world of growing secularism,
the faith in Ireland was perceived as having
remained a comforting constant.

Dermot Keogh

In June 2021 the *Irish Examiner* published a two-page special report by Liz Dunphy on women who had suffered grievously because of the scandals of the Magdalene laundries and symphysiotomy under the heading 'Survivors of a theocratic Ireland'.[1]

The sense that Ireland was a theocracy in all but name (the word was never mentioned) for decades after independence has certainly grown as a fuller picture of the terrible abuse and violation of human rights in the horrific institutions such as the laundries, the industrial schools and the mother and baby homes emerged.

A theocracy is a contested description, of course. When my book *Has God Logged Off?* was published in 2008, it included this sentence: 'Yes, I'm groping toward it: the Ireland in which I grew up was, in effect, a theocracy.' In a subsequent review (a very fair one) of the book by my former *Irish Press* colleague Mary Kenny, she took exception to this passage.

---

1   *Irish Examiner*, 29 June 2021.

He wonders, did we live in a theocracy then? No, TP, we didn't. A theocracy is a country in which there is no freedom of worship for other denominations: no division in law between Church and State: and an ecclesiastical police ensuring that State religion is enforced in public and private.[2]

I wonder now, though, given all that we additionally know in the thirteen years since my book was published, if Mary Kenny would be quite so assertive in denying that Ireland was a theocracy.

If we look at the dictionary definition of theocracy – 'form of government by God or God directly or through a priestly order' (*Oxford Dictionary of Current English*) or 'government by a deity or a priesthood' (*Collins English Dictionary*) – we are closer to the reality on the ground in Ireland from 1922 up to 1960 at least in terms of the influence and control exercised by a priesthood acting in the name of a deity. The sense of this reality was aptly captured by the oft-repeated expression that Ireland for a long time was governed not from Leinster House but from Maynooth.

There may have been a division in law between Church and State, but, even now, in 2022, that hasn't translated into real separation (just consider the ongoing controversy over the National Maternity Hospital, the Catholic control of education, or the manner in which the misplaced loyalty to Pope Paul VI's 1968 encyclical *Humanae vitae* continues to distort and impoverish the Church's sex education programme).

Okay, we did not have the kind of full-blown, all-encompassing theocracy that operates in a place like Saudi Arabia. And, on balance, describing Ireland as a theocracy is an overstatement. But the fusion of Catholicism and nationalism and all that flowed from that, and the handing over by successive governments of responsibility (with no accountability) for key areas of Irish life to the Catholic Church amounted to at the very least a partial theocracy. Nowhere was this more obvious than in the sphere of human sexuality.

Anne Harris, the former editor of the *Sunday Independent*, made the interesting observation that Irish theocracy was voluntary. 'Nobody

---

2   *The Irish Catholic*, 1 January 2009.

forced it on us. That same voluntary theocracy which saw families reject their pregnant daughters, also sent their sons to be priests aged eight, and daughters with no vocations to be nuns,' she wrote.[3]

The scandal of the mother and baby homes testifies to this notion of 'voluntary' theocracy. When I was growing up you would hear occasional muted comments among adults about Bessborough (a notorious mother and baby home in Blackrock in Cork city). People knew what was going on in Bessborough, but such was the opprobrium attached to girls who gave birth outside wedlock that it suited the community to have places where they could be hidden away, kept out of sight of 'respectable' society. Whether the theocracy was voluntary or involuntary, what matters was the reality of it, partial or otherwise. The other side of it was the off-loading of moral responsibility that it facilitated.

Any mention of 'theocracy', of course, will annoy some people, not least politicians who would insist that they were in control, they were calling the shots, not kowtowing to stern-faced clerics. But at what point does the ceding of control by selected representatives, or the abdication of responsibility on their part, start to shade into theocracy?

In his acclaimed book *Moral Monopoly*, Tom Inglis of UCD brilliantly demonstrates how the Catholic Church in Ireland came to gain a monopoly over morality. One passage is illustrative:

> The process of incorporating Catholic teaching in Irish legislation, which began shortly after the foundation of the Free State, reached a peak with the passing of the Irish Constitution of 1937. The Constitution strongly represents Catholic moral teaching, especially with regard to family, private property and education … The social legislation of the 1920s and 1930s, followed by the Constitution, set a precedent by which the hierarchy seemed to have the right and duty to limit the State when it came to legislation involving moral issues. But there were many pieces of legislation which involved moral issues of some kind and, at the height of their power in the 1950s, some bishops came close to advocating

3   In a Rite & Reason column in the *Irish Times*, 29 June 2021.

a theocratic state. This is best illustrated by a statement from the Bishop of Cork, Dr Lucey. Referring to the Health Bill of 1953, he noted that 'their [the bishops] position was that they were the final arbiters of right and wrong even in political matters'.[4]

This situation arose because of what Dermot Keogh, professor emeritus of Irish history at UCC, called a special alliance between Church and State. In 1988, in a Thomas Davis Lecture on the background to the drafting of the 1937 Constitution, Keogh had emphasised the Catholic ethos within which this occurred.

> The central role of Catholicism in the political life of the new state must be kept to the fore. The influence of individual clergymen in the drafting of the 1937 Constitution must be set in that context. By the 1930s, Catholicism had become the central characteristic of Irish nationalism ... The Eucharistic Congress in 1932 demonstrated the central importance of Catholicism in the celebration of national identity. On that occasion, Faith and Fatherland were as one.[5]

The practical implications of this special alliance between religion and politics were detailed by Louise Fuller of NUI Maynooth in her 2004 book, *Irish Catholicism Since 1950*, and referenced earlier in this book. Fuller was quick to emphasise the wider acceptance of this special alliance.

> It is important to bear in mind that the kind of loyalty towards, and legitimisation of, Catholicism by politicians in the post-independent era was totally in keeping with the thinking and lifestyle of the vast majority of the Catholic population of the Republic of Ireland in the 1950s.[6]

---

4   Tom Inglis, *Moral Monopoly: The Rise and Fall of the Catholic Church in Modern Ireland* (Dublin: University College Dublin Press, 1998), pp. 79–80.

5   Dermot Keogh, 'Church, State and Society' in Brian Farrell, ed., *De Valera's Constitution and Ours* (Dublin: Gill and Macmillan, 1988), p. 105.

6   Louise Fuller, *Irish Catholicism Since 1950: The Undoing of a Culture* (Dublin: Gill and Macmillan, 2004), p. 19.

The interpenetration of Church and State suited both sides. 'From the early days, the government proved willing to use the power of the State to protect Catholic moral values,' according to JH Whyte in his ground-breaking book, *Church and State in Modern Ireland 1923–1979.*[7]

The State was content to outsource public health services, including control of hospitals which it funded, as well as education, to the Church. The long-running controversy over the National Maternity Hospital was rightly described by an editorial in the *Irish Times* as 'a symptom of a bigger problem.'[8] That bigger problem was the ready acceptance for far too long, and not just of an acceptance but a complicity, in an Irish form of 'political religion'.

The use of moral authority by the Church to influence policy in Ireland was greatly facilitated by the passivity of Catholics in general, including the deferential (some would say supine) attitude of Catholic politicians towards the clerical establishment.

---

7   JH Whyte, *Church and State in Modern Ireland 1923–1979* (Dublin: Gill and Macmillan, 1980) (2nd edn), p. 36.

8   *The Irish Times*, 22 June 2021.

Chapter 10

IMAGINE

The world today is massively religious,
and is anything but the secularised
world that had been predicted.

Peter L. Berger

In the decades since the release of John Lennon's 'Imagine' as a single in Britain in October 1975, the world has undergone enormous changes. One of the most significant changes was the fall of the Berlin Wall in November 1989. This paved the way for German reunification in October 1990 and, in turn, triggered the dissolution of the Soviet Union in December 1991.

In 1992, in the aftermath of the implosion of the Soviet Union, the American political scientist Francis Fukuyama of Stanford University was quick off the mark with his book *The End of History* in which he predicted the triumph of liberalism as well as secularisation. However, it hasn't quite worked out like that – not for liberalism and certainly not for secularisation.

The horrific events of 9/11, the perpetrators of which were religiously motivated, put a bloody end to all talk of the 'end of history'. The destruction of the World Trade Center also raised again, though with a new and sudden urgency, old questions, mainly about the role of religion.

In view of all that has happened, why does anyone need religion in the twenty-first century? And why do so many people across the globe still claim a religious affiliation of one sort or another? Surely in these more secular times we should be seeing an abandonment of religion.

Questions such as these surface from time to time in discussions on radio and television about the persistence of religion, or when the differences between Christianity and Islam are being talked about. These days, nobody pretends that religion doesn't matter.

It was Karl Marx (1818–83) who popularised the idea of religion as a crutch, something that gives false comfort. He called it 'the opiate of the poor'. However, as broadcaster John Humphrys has emphasised, for vast numbers of ordinary, thoughtful people it is impossible not to believe in God. 'Quite simply – and this will cause many an atheist lip to curl – they *want* there to be something else.'[1]

But what if there isn't something else? What if there is no heaven, or no hell? In July 2001, on the day that Liverpool Airport was being renamed the John Lennon Airport, his widow Yoko Ono made this comment to those attending the ceremony: 'As John said, there is no hell below us, and above us only sky.'

This statement of unbelief in the supernatural had a powerful resonance for many young people, a tribute among other things to the powerful influence of a musical and cultural icon.

In January 2001 the *Observer* published the results of a poll conducted in cooperation with Channel 4 to find the '100 Greatest Number 1 Singles'. The winner was John Lennon's 'Imagine', recorded at the home of the best and most richly gifted of the Beatles in Ascot in May 1971, though not released as a single until October 1975. In an 'anatomy of an anthem', Yoko Ono said: 'We both felt that it was an important song ... the song was more like a prayer than a prediction: a prayer in the sense of "Let's hope that this will circulate".'

The result of the poll was hardly a surprise. 'With its utopian sentiments, solemn piano coda and wistful lyrics, "Imagine" has become the premier item in pop's slim hymnal, edging McCartney's "Let It Be" into second place, with Simon and Garfunkel's "Bridge Over Troubled Waters" among the also rans,' wrote Neil Spencer in the *Observer's* commentary on the poll.

---

1 John Humphrys, *In God We Doubt: Confessions of a Failed Athiest* (London: Hodder and Stoughton, 2007), p. 17.

'Imagine' is anti-religion, anti-nationalism, anti-capitalism and anti-conformity. For these sentiments, plus its inherent musical qualities, it had and still has huge appeal, especially among the disenchanted and rebellious young. It is a blueprint for a utopia that hitherto only writers of science fiction had speculated about. In the course of the song Lennon concedes that critics of the message of the lyrics may dismiss him as 'a dreamer', but most assuredly, as he was quick to add in the recording, he is 'not the only one'.

In a post-9/11 world, where we have witnessed the emergence (or re-emergence) of 'politicised' religion, very many people must, from time to time, have felt that the world would be a far better place if all religions were abolished. Many of them do not accept, as popes would have us all accept, that a world without God is a world without hope.

These days a new generation of disaffected youth – deeply sceptical of conventional religion, anti-Church, anti-establishment, anti-war, anti-hypocrisy, anti-globalisation – readily embrace the idealism of 'Imagine'. Never mind the irony of the admonition to 'imagine no possessions' coming from a millionaire rock star, or the fact that one of Lennon's most scabrous critics, the author Albert Goldman (best known for a controversial 1981 biography of Elvis Presley), has dismissed 'Imagine' as a 'hippie wishing-list full of pennyweight dreams for a better world'. In spite of this, the song is still regarded by the young as an anthem of hope, an anthem full of promise, resonating with the vision of an alternative world, a war-free, greed-free, conflict-free and, yes, a God-free world.

It is easy to be cynical in an age when cynicism is a synonym for cool, but Lennon believed in the possibility of a better world. Such is the status and influence of rock stars today that he may well have inspired millions of young people to believe in such a possibility as well. And that is no bad thing.

In the forty-five years since its release as a single in Britain, Lennon's vision of a Godless, secularised society has been realised to a considerable extent in parts of the Western world in particular. However, the overall impact of the process of secularisation on the religious landscape globally has been less than many predicted or others hoped for.

The American philosopher Sam Harris (*The End of Faith*) is one of the best-known of the New Atheists along with Richard Dawkins (*The God*

Delusion) and Christopher Hitchens (*God Is Not Great*) whose books have sold in huge numbers. Yet, in his 2010 book, Harris felt compelled to make this admission:

> Since the nineteenth century, it has been widely assumed that the spread of industrialised society would spell the end of religion. Marx, Freud and Weber – along with innumerable anthropologists, sociologists, historians, and psychologists influenced by their work – expected religious belief to wither in the light of modernity. It has not come to pass. Religion remains one of the most important aspects of human life in the twenty-first century ... When one considers the rise of Islamism throughout the Muslim world, the explosive spread of Pentecostalism throughout Africa, and the anomalous piety of the United States, it becomes clear that religion will have geopolitical consequences for a long time to come.[2]

That same year, John Micklethwait and Adrian Wooldridge produced *God is Back: How the Global Rise of Faith is Changing the World*. That said it all. Lennon's dream had been buried in the rubble of the World Trade Center.

---

2   Sam Harris, *The Moral Landscape: How Science can Determine Human Values* (London: Bantam Press, 2010), p. 145.

Chapter 11

RELIGION AND POLITICS

Christianity, Judaism and Buddhism
have all made significant contributions
to mainstream politics.

Alain de Botton

The links, or interrelationships, between religion and politics have a long and sometimes contentious history, as we have seen. Down the ages the politicisation of religion has been a constant and recurring reality in our world.

'Religion continues to be a vehicle for political expression and change, whether peaceful or violent, in a way surprising to those who once expected a progressive secularisation ultimately to reach every part of the globe,' Martin Woollacott emphasised in an article entitled 'In the name of God, why are we fighting?'[1]

Writing on 'Religion and Politics', Robert Pope, senior lecturer in theology, University of Wales, sketches a picture providing the necessary context and background.

The common perception in the West is that religion and politics should not mix. This is largely the result of the eighteenth-century

---

1   *The Sydney Morning Herald*, 11 December 2002.

Enlightenment, since which it has become common to argue that as a society modernises so it becomes secular and disentangled from dependence on God. Human ability to control and exploit the environment through scientific and technological advance meant that the formal reliance on God to provide protection, shelter and sustenance was no longer necessary. The consequent separation of Church (as the custodian of the sacred) and State (as the political community) is a specifically Western and modern idea, stemming more from secular philosophy than from religious understanding. Although it has won widespread acceptance, such a simplistic separation between religion and politics can be seen to be ideological and historically mistaken.[2]

Pope goes on to emphasise that in the present day, religious practitioners have held a tremendous influence on Western democracies and governments elsewhere through agitating on moralistic and nationalistic issues.

'Throughout history, then, religion and politics have maintained a complex, if increasingly ambivalent, relationship.' The potency of that relationship, especially when it involves radical Islam, is better appreciated than it was fifty years ago.

'Perhaps more than any other religion, Islam has been criticised for its political associations and the willingness of its most militant followers to engage in extreme measures to achieve their goals,' Pope points out. 'The dangers of this are only too evident following the attack on the World Trade Center on 11 September 2001. As a result of this, the concern of many that religion and politics held too close an association has, to an extent, given way to the fear that religion has too close an association with terrorism.'[3]

But if religion harms, it also heals. Avowed atheist Alain de Botton provides one of the best justifications for religion in an intriguing and well-written book called *Religion for Atheists*.[4] It is true that his argument is a

---

2   Robert Pope, 'Religion and Politics' in Christopher Partridge, ed., *The World's Religions* (Oxford: Lion, 2005), p. 453.

3   Ibid., p. 455.

4   Alain de Botton, *Religion for Atheists: A Non-Believer's Guide to the Uses of Religion* (London: Hamish Hamilton, 2012).

utilitarian one, and he highlights the positive aspects of religion in a context where they are sundered from any supernatural superstructure.

> One can be left cold by the doctrines of the Christian Trinity and the Buddhist Eightfold Path and yet at the same time be interested in the ways in which religions deliver sermons, promote morality, engender a spirit of community, make use of art and architecture, inspire travels, train minds and encourage gratitude at the beauty of spring. In a world beset by fundamentalists of both believing and secular varieties, it must be possible to balance a rejection of religious faith with a selective reverence for religious rituals and concepts.
>
> It is when we stop believing that religions have been handed down from above or else that they are entirely daft that matters become more interesting. We can then recognise that we invented religion to serve two central needs which continue to this day and which secular society has not been able to solve with any particular skill: first, the need to live together in communities in harmony, despite our deeply rooted selfish and violent impulses. And second, the need to cope with terrifying degrees of pain which arise from our vulnerability to professional failure, to troubled relationships, to the death of loved ones and to our decay and demise. God may be dead, but the urgent issues which impelled us to make him up still stir and demand resolutions which do not go away when we have been nudged to perceive some scientific inaccuracies in the tale of seven loaves and fishes.
>
> The error of modern atheism has been to overlook how many aspects of the faiths remain relevant even after their central tenets have been dismissed. Once we cease to feel that we must either prostrate ourselves before them or denigrate them, we are free to discover religions as repositories of a myriad ingenious concepts with which we can try to assuage a few of the more persistent and unattended ills of secular life.[5]

---

5   Ibid., pp. 12–13.

De Botton contends that secular society has been unfairly impoverished by the loss of an array of practices and themes which atheists typically find impossible to live with because they seem too closely associated with the 'bad odours of religion' (to quote Nietzsche).

> We have grown frightened of the word *morality*. We bridle at the thought of hearing a sermon. We flee from the idea that art should be uplifting or have an ethical mission. We don't go on pilgrimages. We can't build temples. We have no mechanisms for expressing gratitude. The notion of reading a self-help book has become absurd to the high-minded. We resist mental exercises. Strangers rarely sing together. We are presented with an unpleasant choice between either committing to peculiar concepts about immaterial deities or letting go entirely of a host of consoling, subtle or just charming rituals for which we struggle to find equivalents in secular society.[6]

He argues that religions merit our attention for their sheer conceptual ambition; for changing the world in a way that few secular institutions ever have.

De Botton rightly focuses on one of the great weaknesses of modern society: 'One of the losses modern society feels most keenly is that of a sense of community.' This is something the late Garret FitzGerald (a former taoiseach) wrote about not long before his death. Instead of writing about a 'loss of sense of community', however, Dr FitzGerald wrote about 'a striking absence of a sense of civic responsibility throughout our entire society', which, of course, had a very corrosive effect on any sense of the common good. Instead of advocating civil responsibility, Dr FitzGerald noted the Catholic Church concentrated much of its energy instead on aspects of sexual morality.[7]

De Botton identifies the privatisation of religion as a major contributory factor in the loss of community.

---

6   Ibid., p. 14.
7   *The Irish Times*, 9 April 2011.

In attempting to understand what could have eroded our sense of community, an important role has traditionally been accorded to the privatisation of religion that occurred in Europe and the United States in the nineteenth century. Historians have suggested that we began to disregard our neighbours at around the same time as we ceased communally to honour our gods. This begs the question of what religions might have done, prior to that time, to enhance the spirit of community, and, more practically, whether secular society could ever recover this spirit without relying on the theological superstructure with which it was once entwined. Could it be possible to reclaim a sense of community without having to base it on religious foundations?[8]

---

8   De Botton, *Religion for Atheists*, pp. 23–4.

Chapter 12

MIXED DOUBLES

The religious faith of leaders is not
to be underestimated. It can drive some to war,
others to peace; some left, some right.

Eliza Filby

There was surprise in Hollywood when Jean Seberg was chosen for the lead role in Otto Preminger's 1957 big-screen adaptation of George Bernard Shaw's great play *Saint Joan*. In French cinematic circles the surprise was mixed with dismay that an American actress had been selected to play one of the country's national icons. Seberg's age – she was just a month short of her eighteenth birthday – wasn't a factor – Joan of Arc was only nineteen when she was burned at the stake in Rouen on 30 May 1431 – but her inexperience was. The film wasn't a critical success, but it – like the original play (the most recent London production of which was in 2016, starring actress Gemma Arterton) – introduced the exploits and trial of the warrior-saint to a new generation.

Today in Paris there is an imposing thirteen-foot gilded bronze equestrian statue of Joan of Arc by Emmanuel Frémiet in Place des Pyramides, not far from the Louvre. Commissioned by the government after the defeat of the country in the 1870 Franco-Prussian War, it was erected in 1874. Once a year, far-right groups hold a rally there, honouring the Maid of Orleans as an ultranationalist and defender of French sovereignty. The Left honours her as a champion of liberty, one of the three stated ideals of the French Revolution.

Euan Ferguson, in his review of the 2015 BBC documentary 'Joan of Arc: God's Warrior', emphasised the conclusion of Helen Castor (author of a biography of Joan) that 'the immense power of faith to move armies, for high good or great evil, is just as urgently relevant in 2015 as it was in 1431'.[1]

A headline over a story in *National Geographic* magazine in 2017 succinctly explained why the young girl from Lorraine was the most important woman of the fifteenth century: 'How Joan of Arc Turned the Tide in the Hundred Years' War'.[2]

There are two statues to Mother Teresa of Calcutta (now Kolkata) – one in Italy and one in Skopje where she was born – and her legion of admirers no doubt feel that she is worthy of them. However, that is far from being a universal view, even among Catholics. She is revered by many, but she also has her critics. The most acerbic was Christopher Hitchens who, in his book *The Missionary Position*, described her as 'a fanatic, a fundamentalist and a fraud'.

Much nearer home, Carol Hunt – writing a year before Mother Teresa's canonisation on 4 September 2016 – said the truth about the Albanian-born nun should not be hidden in misty-eyed romanticism. 'Evidence – and her own words – show that Mother Teresa was not so much a "champion of the poor" but a religious fanatic who took pleasure in their suffering. Not only did she refuse to alleviate the pain of her patients but she gloried in it.'[3]

As both women are embodiments, in their very different ways, of 'political religion', I thought I should include them in a list of 'pairings' I was preparing, but then decided against it.

There is also the example of the former archbishop of Cape Town, Desmond Tutu (who died on 26 December 2021), often looked upon as a political agitator as much as a churchman for his role in ending the apartheid regime in South Africa. Nelson Mandela once called him the 'voice of the voiceless'.

In the next four chapters, the focus will be on eight other high-profile public figures (including some major religious figures) – seven of which are

---

1   *The Observer*, 31 May 2015.
2   *National Geographic*, 21 April 2017.
3   *The Sunday Independent*, 20 December 2015.

from the twentieth century. The exception is Martin Luther whose 'protest' in 1517 started the Reformation. The eight are paired and profiled, with the aim being to show political religion at work in and through their roles and influence. In other words, it is an attempt to put 'flesh and blood' on what might otherwise be considered abstract and theoretical material.

There is something quite arbitrary about the four pairings (mixed doubles) which follow on from this chapter. It very much reflects my personal choices or preferences. Others no doubt would opt for different pairings; there is certainly no shortage of suitable candidates. The list of pairings I have settled on is:

- Francis Spellman and John Charles McQuaid
- Ian Paisley and Karol Wojtyła
- Martin Luther and Dietrich Bonhoeffer
- Dorothy Day and Margaret Thatcher

In drawing up my list I wanted to choose major religious and/or political figures who would be seen as representing the very embodiment of political religion (or faith-based politics).

While the list is arbitrary, there is also a certain connectedness about the pairings, more obvious perhaps in some cases than in others. This connectedness may stem from the fact that the individuals in some pairings complement each other (Spellman and McQuaid being the most obvious example), while in other cases it is the very sharpness of the contrast that is striking (Dorothy Day and Margaret Thatcher).

Originally, I drew up a list of twenty pairings. It soon became apparent that this was far too many and would merely lead me into needless repetition. Among those I eliminated were Muhammad and Calvin, Cardinal Paul Cullen, Archbishop Daniel Mannix, Angela Merkel (whose father was a Protestant pastor, something she has in common with another formidable politician, Margaret Thatcher, whose father was a lay preacher in the local Methodist church in Grantham; this was a role the young Margaret would also take on), and Sophie Scholl, the young Christian girl from Munich University who was executed in 1943 by the Nazis along with two other students from the White Rose resistance movement.

They had fought against Hitler's tyranny, as Sophie's biographer Frank McDonough emphasised, 'not with bullets and bombs, but with words, printed in leaflets, that proclaimed a passionate desire to live in a free and democratic society'.

The Russian Patriarch, Kirill I, will be referenced later on, notably because of the role of the Russian Orthodox Church in supporting and aligning itself with the regime of Vladimir Putin.

I could have included the Abbe Emmanuel-Joseph Sieyès after my friend and former colleague for many years on the religion beat, John Cooney, pointed out in an email that my preliminary list contained no figure from the French Revolution, 'which became anti-Christian and which is such a pivotal event for the shaping of the papacy's opposition to liberalism up to Vatican II'. He suggested Robespierre and the Abbe Sieyès and, after some reflection, I opted for neither.

Sieyès, churchman (he was ordained in 1772 and became chancellor of the Diocese of Chartres in 1788) and constitutional theorist, became famous with the publication of his pamphlet 'What Is the Third Estate?' in January 1789. It led to the formation of a national assembly, so initiating the French Revolution. He helped to draft the *Declaration of the Rights of Man and the Citizen* (26 August 1789), which became a cornerstone document of the French Revolution – and, according to some historians, its greatest legacy. Sieyès also helped to plan the *coup d'etat* that brought Napoleon Bonaparte to power in 1799. He was certainly, even more so than Robespierre, a formidable exponent of political religion.

John also questioned the pairing of Spellman and McQuaid, pointing out that 'they are too alike as authoritarian ultramontanes and shadowy sexual deviants'. But it is precisely because they were such dominant and effective representatives and practitioners of political religion in their respective jurisdictions (and also near-contemporaries) that I kept them paired. John also said that because Spellman was 'very much associated with jingoistic militarism in Vietnam' (and I agree wholeheartedly), I should contrast him with the Jesuit priest Daniel Berrigan. When Berrigan died in 2016, this was the first paragraph of a lengthy obituary in the *Guardian*: 'The American Jesuit priest Father Daniel Berrigan, who has died aged ninety-four, formed a radical partnership with his younger brother, Philip, that energised the movement against the Vietnam War in the 1960s and created a tradition of pacifist activism that lasted a generation'.[4]

I would readily admit that Dan Berrigan would have to be included in any list of those for whom political religion was a lived reality, just as would Rev. Jerry Falwell (a television evangelist who founded the Moral Majority lobby in 1979, credited with getting Ronald Reagan elected in 1980), though operating to a very different agenda than Berrigan's, but I decided to settle on Dorothy Day as my twentieth-century female American representative.

Another very good friend, Margaret Mansfield, suggested Pope Urban II (1088–99), who at the Synod of Clermont issued a summons to the First Crusade (1095–9) on 27 November 1095, calling on Christians to deliver Jerusalem from Muslim dominance. Margaret said this made him 'the first jihadi pope'. That's a reasonable point, but I decided to pass on Urban II, having already decided to include one much more modern pope.

Early on I had pencilled in the name 'Roncalli' who, as Pope John XXIII, had convened the Second Vatican Council (1962–5), the most important religious event of the twentieth century. Then I baulked, as almost any pope could be included in a list like mine because all popes are 'political' by virtue of the nature of their office. If I merely concentrated on popes I'd be embarking on a very different sort of book. Then there is this question: was Vatican I (1869–70) a more 'political' council than Vatican II?

I was also conscious that while John XXIII had specified that *aggiornamento* (updating) was one of the main themes of the Council, he died on 3 June 1963 after just the first session, with three more to follow. The two main documents interfacing with the world – the *Pastoral Constitution on the Church in the Modern World* and the *Declaration on Religious Liberty* – weren't promulgated by his successor, Paul VI, until 7 December 1965, the day before the Council formally ended.

---

4   *The Guardian*, 2 May 2016.

Chapter 13

GOD'S POLITICIANS:
SPELLMAN AND McQUAID

The subject of religion and politics conjures
powerful emotions for and against.

Francis Fukuyama

Cardinal Francis Spellman, who was archbishop of New York from 1939 to 1967, once declared that all serving US troops in Vietnam were 'soldiers of Christ'. And at a military base outside Saigon he was photographed blessing tanks and aircraft, sprinkling them with holy water. Fidel Castro would later refer to him, after the Bay of Pigs invasion of April 1961, as 'the cardinal of the Pentagon, the CIA and the North American monopolies'.

Spellman was a hugely influential figure, not just within the American Church but in the Vatican and Washington DC as well. He had a wide range of contacts and was befriended by presidents as well as popes. 'He was not only the Church's chief political voice, but also the Church's primary kingmaker in America,' according to one of his biographers.[1] His protégés came to be known as 'Spellman's boys', and they moved into positions of responsibility and power not just in New York but across the nation.

---

1   John Cooney, *The American Pope: The Life and Times of Francis Cardinal Spellman* (New York: Times Books, 1984), p. 248.

As Cooney says, Spellman made his imprint on much of the rest of the country. 'This would be felt for decades in a rigid conservatism that supported war and nuclear weapons while opposing activism that might redress societal inequities.'[2]

In Ireland the term of office of John Charles McQuaid as archbishop of Dublin coincided almost exactly with that of Spellman's. McQuaid was appointed in 1940, just one year after Spellman, and over the next three decades became the dominant figure in the Irish Catholic Church. The description of him in the subtitle of John Cooney's excellent biography – *John Charles McQuaid: Ruler of Catholic Ireland* – aptly sums up the influence he wielded.[3] Even before his appointment as archbishop, that influence was making itself felt. McQuaid became president of Blackrock College in Dublin (an institution run by the Holy Ghost Fathers, the order into which he was ordained in 1924) and by then he was already on very friendly terms with the politician who would become the other dominant leader of post-independent Ireland – Éamon de Valera (who had been educated in Blackrock College), the future taoiseach and, later, president of Ireland. That friendship would see McQuaid playing an important role in the shaping of *Bunreacht na hÉireann*, the new constitution that de Valera was determined to bring into being to replace the hated Free State Constitution of 1922. The 1937 document, while it did not describe Catholicism as the State religion (to the disappointment of the Vatican), did ascribe a 'special position' to the Catholic Church in Article 44 (this was deleted in 1972). The document itself was described as 'institutionalising a powerful Catholic ethos that was symbolically celebrated in the Eucharistic Congress of 1932, and effectively enshrined in the Constitution of 1937'.[4]

John A. Murphy of UCC said, 'In many respects the Constitution bore a specifically Catholic complexion, expressing the values of a homogeneously Catholic Twenty-Six County society.'[5]

McQuaid was described by UCD historian Diarmaid Ferriter as 'a man of exceptional talent, cunning, faith and ruthlessness'. He goes on to say that

---

2   Ibid., p. 248.

3   John Cooney, *John Charles McQuaid: Ruler of Catholic Ireland* (Dublin: The O'Brien Press, 1999).

4   RF Foster, *Modern Ireland 1600–1972* (London: Penguin Books, 1989), p. 537.

5   John A. Murphy, *Ireland in the Twentieth Century* (Dublin: Gill and Macmillan, 1975), p. 91.

McQuaid 'was for many the ultimate symbol of clerical domination of Irish life' throughout the three decades from 1940 to 1972. 'His advice was given whether sought or not, and he had a direct line to government which was unsurprising given that his appointment had been championed by both the Taoiseach and Papal Nuncio.'[6]

McQuaid was as virulently anti-Communist as Spellman, having imbibed Pope Pius XI's strictures against 'atheistic communism' outlined in the 1937 encyclical *Divini Redemptoris*. In 1957, after Frank Aiken, Irish minister for external affairs, controversially backed a motion supporting a discussion of China's membership of the United Nations (defying pressure from Washington), the Irish bishops wrote a letter of protest to the government saying the move 'did not reflect the views of Irish Catholics'. McQuaid, who was furious, forwarded the letter to Spellman, who was even more furious. Later, at a lunch hosted by Spellman in New York and attended by Aiken and Frederick Boland, Ireland's Ambassador to the UN, a 'flaming row ensued' over any recognition of Red China.[7]

In 1959 McQuaid, as Mary Kenny reminded her readers, had actually 'tried to ban Dubliners from watching a football match with Communist Yugoslavia, inspired by such demons as Marx'.[8] A decade previously McQuaid was well aware of the Communist challenge. Prior to the 1948 general election in Italy, when there was a real fear, not least in the Vatican, that the Italian Left would gain power, various pleas for financial assistance for the Christian Democrats were made. McQuaid was to the fore. Irish Catholics sent over £60,000 to Rome. 'The Archbishop of Dublin was the largest contributor: McQuaid collected £40,500,' according to Dr Dermot Keogh of UCC.[9]

McQuaid's finest hour, fully justifying his biographer's description of him as 'Ecclesiastical Taoiseach', was his involvement in the Mother and Child controversy of 1950–1 when an inter-party government led by John A. Costello was in power.

---

6   Diarmaid Ferriter, *The Transformation of Ireland 1900–2000* (London: Profile Books, 2005), pp. 411–12.

7   Cooney, *John Charles McQuaid*, p. 330.

8   Mary Kenny, *Goodbye to Catholic Ireland* (London: Sinclair-Stevenson, 1997), p. 254.

9   Dermot Keogh, *Ireland and the Vatican: The Politics and Diplomacy of Church–State Relations, 1922–1960* (Cork: Cork University Press, 1995), p. 245.

In his acclaimed book on Church–State relations, JH Whyte of Queen's University put the controversy, in which McQuaid was a key player, in context: 'Of all the issues which ruffled the course of Church–State relations during the first inter-party government, the most serious was the crisis over mother and child health services'.[10]

A very young and idealistic minister for health, Dr Noël Browne, was determined to introduce a free scheme of antenatal and postnatal care for mothers, as well as free medical care for all children under sixteen. He wanted no means-test included in the mother-and-child section of the 1947 Health Act. This alarmed not just the medical profession, worried about a loss of revenue, but also the Catholic hierarchy. Talk of 'socialised medicine' and the imposition of a 'welfare state' abounded.

In their letter to the Taoiseach, the bishops said the scheme 'contained provision for the physical education of children and for the education of mothers. These were matters in which the State had no competence. Furthermore, they could cover topics – such as birth control and abortion – on which the Catholic Church has definite teaching. There was no guarantee in the scheme that this teaching would be respected.'[11]

It remains, as historian JJ Lee has emphasised, 'one of the great *cause célèbres* of Irish politics'.[12] John Cooney says that McQuaid, in a letter to the Papal Nuncio, four days after Dr Browne's resignation as minister for health, 'boasted that the hierarchy's condemnation of the Mother and Child Scheme and the condemnation of it by the inter-party government led by Taoiseach John A. Costello, was the most important event in Irish history since Daniel O'Connell had achieved Catholic Emancipation in 1829'.[13]

Conor Cruise O'Brien, who was in the Department of External Affairs at the time, said the Costello–MacBride government was 'about to crash in a major crisis over Church–State relations: the greatest such crisis to occur in Ireland since the fall of Charles Stewart Parnell in 1891'.[14]

---

10   JH Whyte, *Church and State in Modern Ireland 1923–1979* (Dublin: Gill and Macmillan, 1980) (2nd edn), p. 196.

11   Ibid., p. 214.

12   JJ Lee, *Ireland 1912–1985: Politics and Society* (Cambridge: Cambridge University Press, 1989), p. 313.

13   Cooney, *John Charles McQuaid*, p. 252.

14   Conor Cruise O'Brien, *Memoir: My Life and Themes* (Dublin: Poolbeg Press, 1999), p. 153.

The Mother and Child controversy, far more than other episodes in Church–State relations, attracted enormous publicity. This followed Dr Browne's action, after his forced resignation, in publishing the correspondence between the bishops, himself and the government. It appeared in three newspapers, the *Irish Independent*, the *Irish Times* and the *Irish Press*.

'Such a move was unprecedented,' noted Louise Fuller. 'For the first time in the history of the independent state, the role of the Church was under public scrutiny.'[15]

The following day, an editorial in the *Irish Times* observed that: 'The Roman Catholic Church would seem to be the effective government of the country'.[16]

Hyperbole aside, it was a hugely important chapter in Church–State relations in Ireland, a potent practical demonstration of political religion in action. 'The significance of the controversy has to do with the unique insight it gave into the power of the hierarchy at the time,' according to Fuller.[17]

The episode is also noteworthy because of the deference shown by Taoiseach John A. Costello to Church authorities. 'I am an Irishman second; I am a Catholic first,' he would later tell the Dáil. Fuller has highlighted this: 'John A. Costello in his letter to Archbishop McQuaid, informing him of the government's decision to withdraw the scheme, asserted "the complete willingness to defer to the judgement so given by the hierarchy that the particular scheme in question is opposed to Catholic social teaching".'[18]

Francis Spellman and John Charles McQuaid met for the first time in June 1932 at the opening of the Eucharistic Congress in Dublin. Spellman, who had been ordained in Rome in 1916, was a monsignor attached to the Secretariat of State and had travelled with the Vatican delegation accompanying the papal legate, Cardinal Lorenzo Lauri, who was to open the Congress. In September 1932, Spellman would be consecrated auxiliary bishop of Boston and his rise to great power had begun. In his biography,

---

15   Louise Fuller, *Irish Catholicism Since 1950: The Undoing of a Culture* (Dublin: Gill and Macmillan, 2004), p. 77.

16   *The Irish Times*, 12 April 1951.

17   Fuller, *Irish Catholicism Since 1950*, p. 76.

18   Ibid., p. 76.

John Cooney (not the same Cooney as McQuaid's biographer) tells us that, especially when promoted to New York, Spellman would become 'a whirlwind of anti-Communist activity'. He even cooperated with the FBI (whose director J. Edgar Hoover became a close friend) in a crackdown on labour unions believed to have Communists operating in their ranks.[19] The authors of *Religion and Politics in the United States* painted a similar picture of the Cardinal:

> Intensely anti-Communist, suspicious of the civil rights and labour movements, and a strong advocate of government efforts to prohibit public displays of 'immorality', Spellman forged strong links between the Church and leaders of secular conservative movements. Under his influence, the Catholic hierarchy enthusiastically endorsed the active involvement of the United States in military conflicts wherever communism was thought to be a threat. From Spain in the 1930s through Vietnam in the 1960s, Spellman consistently favoured a policy satirised by the phrase 'Praise the Lord and pass the ammunition'.[20]

Leading American theologian, Charles Curran, suggested the Cardinal's influence in backing the American involvement in Vietnam extended to other members of the hierarchy: 'The vast majority of American bishops favoured the war in the middle 1960s. Cardinal Spellman, archbishop of New York, was the leading spokesperson for this group.'[21]

Writing in his journal in July 1971, following the leaking of the Pentagon Papers to the *New York Times* (and, later, the *Washington Post*), Arthur Schlesinger Jr, JFK's favourite historian, said:

> What the publication does is accentuate the basic mystery: why anyone ever supposed that Vietnam so involved the American national interest or so threatened the security of the United States

---

19   Cooney, *The American Pope*, p. 146.

20   Kenneth D. Wald and Allison Calhoun-Brown, *Religion and Politics in the United States* (New York and Oxford: Rowman and Littlefield, 2007) (5th edn), p. 250.

21   Charles E. Curran, *American Catholic Social Ethics* (Notre Dame and London: University of Notre Dame Press, 1982), p. 237.

as to justify the frightful slaughter and destruction we have brought to this remote and alien country.[22]

Such a consideration – in essence a moral consideration – never seemed to have troubled Spellman. Moreover, pressing social and socio-economic issues, like race, poverty and appalling inequalities so widespread in the USA, never seemed to have engaged him. As Cooney noted at the time of Spellman's seventy-fifth birthday (1964), 'these were topics about which the aged Cardinal was either silent or disdainful'. Yet this was just three years after the publication of the first of Pope John XXIII's great social encyclicals, *Mater et magistra* ('Mother and Teacher'), and a year after the second, *Pacem in terris* ('Peace on Earth').

Spellman, like McQuaid, didn't like Pope John XXIII, and was hostile like his Dublin counterpart to the Second Vatican Council (1962–5), being an 'obstructionist'. Both men were very much out of step with Vatican II from the outset. Before leaving for Rome and the opening of the Council, Spellman vowed that 'no change will get past the Statue of Liberty'. The assurance he gave to American Catholics was echoed in Dublin by McQuaid. In a sermon in the Pro-Cathedral after returning from the Council, he told Irish Catholics: 'Let me reassure you. No change will worry the tranquillity of your Christian lives.'

On 27 December 1971, much to his disappointment and chagrin, McQuaid was informed by the Papal Nuncio that his letter of retirement (required under new Vatican rules) on reaching the age of seventy-five had been accepted by Pope Paul VI. Two years later (7 April 1973), he was dead. The McQuaid era was over. 'His policy was based on the principle that error has no rights, and on his desire to protect his flock from what he considered harmful influences. Such a policy was framed for a static and conservative society,' according to John Cooney.

Dr Noël Browne claimed that the most important development in political life during his episcopacy was the relationship established between himself and de Valera under the 1937 Constitution, when

---

22   Arthur Schlesinger Jr, *Journals 1952–2000* (London: Atlantic Books, 2008), pp. 338–9.

each of them worked together. 'The Church used the State; the State used the Church. This in my view led to the setting up of the sectarian society of the North because of their fear of becoming part of a society which was essentially, as this society had become, a theocratic state in which Catholic law and moral teaching became State law'.[23]

Spellman's jingoism would eventually lead to a rupturing of his relations with the Vatican. On 4 October 1965, Pope Paul VI arrived in New York to address the UN, where he would plead: 'No more war, never again war!' He saw the Vietnam War as a calamity that must be ended, but Spellman was consistently saying that anything less than victory was inconceivable.

> What disturbed the Pope was Spellman's hawkishness on Vietnam while he was quietly trying to work for peace ... The two had had talks about Spellman's support of the US war effort, but Paul's pleas to have Spellman temper his enthusiasm fell on deaf ears. The Vatican was much concerned about Spellman's holding too much power. The money he collected gave him enormous influence, and he still was the military vicar of the US Armed Forces. There was growing sentiment in Rome that the Cardinal of New York should not also be the military vicar; the dual role vested too much authority in one man.[24]

In December 1966, during his Christmas visit to Vietnam, Spellman told the US troops they were 'holy crusaders' engaged in 'Christ's war against the Vietcong'.[25] As the war dragged on, Spellman had his picture taken not simply with generals and GIs but blessing bombers and machine guns.

The Cardinal's bellicosity divided the Catholic community and brought anti-war demonstrators to his residence and to St Patrick's Cathedral. The response of a growing number of priests to his sabre-rattling statements was summarised in a letter to the *New York Times* on

---

23   Cooney, *John Charles McQuaid*, p. 433.
24   Cooney, *The American Pope*, pp. 290–1.
25   Ibid., p. 306.

24 December 1965: 'It looks as if Cardinal Spellman is in Vietnam to bless the guns which the Pope is begging us to put down'. The letter was signed by a New York priest.[26]

> Spellman's Americanism was out of control – the Cardinal had broken with the Pope. From a Vatican perspective, even Spellman's Christmas cards in 1965, the year the Pope negotiated a temporary truce, were an insult. The picture on the cards was of him standing before a fighter plane with two military officers.[27]

Cardinal Spellman died in 1967 at the age of seventy-eight, shortly after being admitted to hospital. 'An era in American Catholicism came to a close on December 2, 1967,' wrote (the other) John Cooney. 'The Spellman legacy of conservative politics, militarism, and pragmatism, however, was so strongly imprinted on the Church that it was to be felt for years to come. The American hierarchy was Spellmanised.'[28]

Both Spellman and McQuaid were consummate ecclesiastical politicians: both understood power and how to use it, and both had a keen appreciation of the relationship between religion and politics, and how the exercise of moral authority could influence public policy, even at the highest levels of the political establishments.

Given that the earthly purpose of organised religion is always, as Deborah Orr wrote, 'the control of attitudes and behaviour',[29] then the realisation of that purpose is greatly facilitated if politics can be harnessed to that endeavour. Down through the ages, ecclesiastical leaders like Spellman and McQuaid have had an acute awareness of this. That's the very essence of political religion. Behind a veneer of civility, both men were exceedingly arrogant, vain, intolerant and self-regarding, and in their respective jurisdictions they took political religion to new heights.

The sexuality of both archbishops has been questioned. 'For years rumours abounded about Cardinal Spellman being a homosexual,' says Cooney.

---

26   Ibid., p. 294.

27   Ibid., p. 294.

28   Ibid., p. 325.

29   *The Guardian*, 19 September 2015.

As a result, many felt – and continue to feel – that Spellman the public moralist may well have been a contradiction of the man of the flesh. Numerous priests and others interviewed took his homosexuality for granted. Others within the Church and outside have steadfastly dismissed such claims … But without question, Spellman was a rabid public moralist. He ranted against movies, plays, and films that treated sex even lightly, let alone those that exploited sexuality as a major theme.[30]

The same was true of McQuaid. 'McQuaid's utter certainty about what was right and wrong led to a preoccupation with the "evils" of sex, reflecting in many ways his own personal repression,' wrote Ferriter.[31] His biographer cites an 'unpublished manuscript by Dr Noël Browne in which he levels a charge against McQuaid of making sexual advances to a schoolboy'.[32] We are told later that Browne 'recoiled from placing the allegation in the public domain because he feared his claim would be treated as an instance of his *animus* against McQuaid'.[33]

Even today, for people of a certain age, as Cooney reminds us, 'the name John Charles McQuaid still conjures up vivid images of a Counter-Reformation prelate ruling the country with an iron will, secure in his knowledge of the divine will'.[34]

Were Spellman and McQuaid practising homosexuals or two prelates with homosexual proclivities? We may never have a definitive answer, but rumours, however persistent, remain just that – rumours. There is no incontrovertible evidence that either man was an active homosexual. Nevertheless, focusing on the sexuality of the two Church leaders is justified precisely because of the position they held and the claims they made in terms of moral leadership and authority. 'The source of Spellman's power was his position as a moral leader of the Church.'[35] What Cooney said of

---

30   Cooney, *The American Pope*, p. 109.

31   Ferriter, *The Transformation of Ireland 1900–2000*, p. 521.

32   Cooney, *John Charles McQuaid*, p. 17.

33   Ibid., p. 287.

34   Ibid., p. 16.

35   Cooney, *The American Pope*, p. 108.

Spellman was equally true of McQuaid. The other Cooney noted that the Archbishop of Dublin, in mid-twentieth-century Ireland, was established as 'the arbiter of public morality in all spheres of human behaviour, particularly sexual conduct'.[36]

To be policing other peoples' morals and acting as the moral arbiter of the public realm, while behaving very differently oneself in private, amounts to rank hypocrisy, and fatally undermines one's moral authority.

---

36   Cooney, *John Charles McQuaid*, p. 277.

Chapter 14

GOD'S POLITICIANS:
PAISLEY AND WOJTYŁA

The Pope goes to his maker
with blood on his hands.

Terry Eagleton

They were both driven by big egos and no small measure of narcissism, and they were both convinced they were doing God's work – *Opus Dei*. It is therefore fitting that Karol Wojtyła and Ian Paisley were contemporaries. Born in Katowice in Poland in 1920, Wojtyła would go on to become the first non-Italian pope for over four hundred and fifty years in 1978. Paisley was born in 1926 in the cathedral town of Armagh in Northern Ireland, and would go on to establish a Church: the Free Presbyterian Church (1951); a newspaper: the *Protestant Telegraph* (1966); and a political party: the Democratic Unionist Party (1971). Overall, his legacy from his ordination on 1 August 1946 up to the Good Friday Agreement of 17 March 1998 was a poisonous one.

The Rev. Ian Kyle Paisley may never have fired a gun, but he employed to deadly effect what the French philosopher Philippe-Joseph Salazar calls 'armed words'.[1] Those words, usually tinged with sectarian hatred, ensure that Paisley looms large in the story of the Northern Ireland Troubles.

---

1   *The Observer*, 29 November 2015.

The Troubles had many causes and more than one contributory factor, but Paisley was very much part of that mix. And a very significant and malevolent part.

In a letter to a newspaper in 2016, journalist Diarmaid MacDermott, whose father was a civil rights activist in Derry, sought to remind readers of the 'real and lasting damage' Paisley's brand of sectarian hatred caused to Ireland in the second half of the twentieth century. 'Paisley's hatred of the Roman Church was the leading factor in his organisation of sectarian hatred against the civil rights movement.' His anti-Romanism 'led directly to the revival of the UVF ... Paisleyism was a sectarian, hate-filled, and anti-Catholic bigoted belief system.'[2]

I first encountered Paisley on one of his anti-Roman crusades in the university town of Uppsala in Sweden in June 1968 where I was covering the month-long Fourth Assembly of the World Council of Churches (WCC) for the *Irish Press*. For the first time since the WCC was founded in 1948, the Vatican had decided to send official observers. At that stage Paisley was still relatively unknown in international circles. But that would soon change.

This was just three years after the end of the Second Vatican Council (1962–5), and its *Decree on Ecumenism* had given a new impetus to the quest for Christian unity. The presence of Vatican observers was further proof of this. In addition, two years previously an event took place which had incensed Paisley: Archbishop of Canterbury Dr Michael Ramsey, representing the Church of England (of which the Queen was supreme governor), had travelled to Rome for an historic meeting with Pope Paul VI.

Paisley and a small group of followers arrived in Uppsala in 1968, brandishing Union Jacks, in what was the first of a series of extraterritorial 'anti-papist' protests culminating in the haranguing of Pope John Paul II during the latter's visit to the European Parliament in 1988. Paisley may have thundered like an Old Testament prophet, but the message he megaphoned was, for too long, one of division and hate.

Paisley was the embodiment of a phenomenon that regularly makes headlines today – mainly because of the volatile and bloody situation in the Middle East – a species of political religion that is extremist in language, precept and form.

2   *The Irish Times*, 6 December 2016.

Through the agency of the Free Presbyterian Church of Ulster, which he established on 17 March 1951, Paisley harnessed religion to the political ideology of hardline, fundamentalist unionism, with far-reaching repercussions for Northern Ireland.

His breakaway from mainstream Presbyterianism on St Patrick's Day 1951 has come to be regarded by some commentators as an event as momentous for those concerned as Luther's public burning of the Pope's edict of excommunication at Wittenberg. It also had dire consequences for the people of Northern Ireland.

The newly founded church would promote a virulent form of anti-Catholicism, demonising the pope as the 'anti-Christ' and opposing all and every manifestation of ecumenism. It was 'free' in the sense that it was no longer subject to any oversight from the mainstream Presbyterian Church.

Paisley would later create another vehicle for the dissemination of a sectarian politico-religious ideology – a newspaper called the *Protestant Telegraph*, which he established in February 1966. The poisonous propaganda that spewed from its pages was a contributory factor to Ed Moloney's conclusion in his biography that Paisley, more than any other single individual, 'brought the Provos into being'.[3]

Paisley became a very potent reminder that politicised religion, which many tend to associate exclusively with the Islamic world, also has Christian roots. Using the Bible to foment hatred of another Christian tradition, convincing Protestant sectarian killers that God is on their side, is something that finds a frightening parallel in the perverted use that the Isis killers made of the Qur'an in Syria and Iraq.

None of this is to deny the presence of a murderous sectarianism with politico-religious roots on the nationalist side throughout the Troubles, even if that side lacked a firebrand evangelical preacher of Paisley's stature. The latter, nevertheless, did his best to cast Tomás Ó Fiaich in that role. When Ó Fiaich – who had been president of Maynooth College – was appointed archbishop of Armagh in October 1977, in succession to Cardinal William Conway, he found himself at the centre of controversy two months later when, in the course of an interview with the *Irish Press*,

---

3   Ed Moloney, *Paisley: From Demagogue to Democrat?* (Dublin: Poolbeg Press, 2008), p. 514.

he said: 'I believe the British should withdraw from Ireland. I think it is the only thing that will get things moving.' It was a comment that provoked Paisley into dubbing him 'the IRA's bishop from Crossmaglen'. Paisley saw the IRA as 'the armed wing of the Roman Catholic Church'.[4]

Leaders of the mainstream Christian churches in the North have always been uneasy with any depiction of the Troubles as a religious war, or even as a war with a religious dimension. Yet the subject matter of Martin Dillon's book, *God and the Gun: The Church and Irish Terrorism*, is sufficient to remove any doubt that extremist political religion was (and remains) an Irish phenomenon that is every bit as destructive as the perverted Islam of al-Qaeda, Boko Haram or Isis.

Madeleine Albright, former US secretary of state during the Clinton presidency, sought to remind us of the role of religion in world affairs: 'We had better accept that the world is filled with political Muslims, political Christians, political Jews, and political people of every other faith. It is no crime to have a political agenda. It is a crime, however, to act on a violent and lawless one'.[5] If the IRA acted on one such agenda, those incited to take up the gun by Paisley's biblically tinged condemnations, demonisations and exhortations acted on another. Of Paisley it was once said that he'd fight to the last drop of someone else's blood. I first heard that description from the late Ciaran McKeown, journalist and one of the founder members of the Peace People.

As we struggle to comprehend the religiously fuelled hatreds that so bedevil the Middle East, we need look no further than Belfast in the period from the mid-1960s to the mid-1990s for clues as to how different tribes of people claiming allegiance to a benevolent God can end up incubating murderous hate for each other.

In an interview with John Humphrys on BBC Radio 4 just short of his eighty-fourth birthday, Paisley was asked how, after all that had happened, he could now be friends with Martin McGuinness: 'I believe God can change people.' If Christianity once brought out the worst in Ian Paisley, we have to acknowledge that in the end it brought out the best in him.

---

4   Ed Moloney, *A Secret History of the IRA* (London: Penguin Books, 2002), p. 233.

5   Madeleine Albright, *The Mighty and the Almighty: Reflections on America, God, and World Affairs* (London: Pan Books, 2007), p. 297.

That said, any attempt to airbrush the early Paisley out of history would do a great disservice to those people who died as a result of the bitterly sectarian political religion he espoused so passionately for so many years. It is no excuse to point to the presence of a 'green' sectarianism on the other side, and certainly no exoneration for the undoubted harm done by Paisley's evangelical fervour mustered in support of a deadly anti-Catholicism.

When asked in that same BBC 4 interview if the Troubles would have been shorter and lives saved if he had stopped saying no earlier and had lent his support to the peace process, Paisley said he didn't accept that. 'Repentance was needed.' That is true, but it was a more all-encompassing repentance than he had in mind.

Ian Paisley's legacy is a very mixed one, and there is a very dark side to it. Of him it could be said, as Tim Pat Coogan, historian and former editor of the *Irish Press* once remarked to me: 'You may not have carried a gun, but your words were certainly weapons!' Did he, I wonder, in his old age, ask himself, in the manner of WB Yeats, if words of his had sent out men to kill?

Eilis O'Hanlon was in no doubt about Paisley's legacy: he was a man, she said, who had stoked vicious sectarian tension in Northern Ireland for decades: 'A Protestant hate-preacher in the mould of Islamic clerics Abu Hamza or Abu Qatada – old men who loved to send out young men to die on their behalf. Innocent men, women and children died because of Paisley's words, but he was showered with sycophantic flattery on his death.'[6] Daniel Geary, associate professor of US history at TCD, situated Paisley's legacy in a wider context in 2018: 'The exclusivist nationalism that Ian Paisley advocated in 1968 lives on in the age of Trump and Brexit.'[7]

Karol Wojtyła was a dictator-pope (not the first by any means), and his finger-wagging episode in Nicaragua in 1983 captured his attitude very well. When John Paul II visited Nicaragua in 1983, he publicly wagged his finger and scolded Fr Ernesto Cardenal as the priest knelt to welcome him at Managua airport. 'You must fix your affairs with the Church,' the Polish Pope told him sternly. In 1979 Cardenal had been named minister of culture in the newly formed left-wing government, a post he would remain in until 1987. It was ironic indeed that he was rebuked for being 'political' by John

---

6   *The Sunday Independent*, 8 October 2017.

7   'Paisley legacy of right-wing ideas lives on in Brexit', *The Irish Times*, 26 September 2018.

Paul II – the most 'political' pope of the twentieth century, with the possible exception of Pius XI, who did a deal with Mussolini.

Wojtyła had one thing in common with Donald Trump – narcissistic authoritarianism. The rush to have him declared a saint after his death in April 2005 was unseemly, to say the least. Now that we know a lot more about his indifference (to put it mildly) to the burgeoning problem of the sexual abuse of children by clergy (including in his native Poland during his time in office), it is surely time for a reappraisal of the second-longest pontificate in the history of the Church (the pontificate of Pius IX, who was pope from 1846 to 1878, is the longest).

In a fiercely critical biography, John Cornwell emphasised that John Paul II had a monarchical image of the papacy, embracing a pyramidal notion of the function of the papacy, as well as promoting the cult of his papal personality which, Cornwell said, 'seemed to encourage an epic self-centredness'.

'John Paul had by the early 1980s revealed himself as an authoritarian rather than a collegial pope; he was inclined to draw the reins of power to the Vatican and to his papal office rather than release authority and local discretion to the dioceses and the local churches.'[8]

Hardly surprising, therefore, that John Paul II had no time for any notions of collegiality. This was one of the key concepts to emerge from Vatican II (1962–5), and refers to a model of Church governance that places a central emphasis on the importance of collaboration between the pope and the bishops of the world (considered as constituting a 'college'). Karol Wojtyła was hostile to this concept: the result was a studied and deliberate reduction in the status of bishops. 'They treat us like altar boys,' the late Cardinal Joseph Bernardin of Chicago once said of John Paul II and the Roman Curia after a visit to the Vatican.

Karol Wojtyła was an autocrat, a showman, and was 'one of the world's leading fundamentalists'. This was how Karen Armstrong, a former nun, described him in a 1994 documentary for Channel 4. The author of several acclaimed books on religion, Armstrong said a desire for absolute certainty in the confusions of the modern world is one of the characteristics of

8   John Cornwell, *The Pope in Winter: The Dark Face of John Paul II's Papacy* (London: Penguin Books, 2005), p. 93.

fundamentalism. 'It springs from a profound fear and rests on the mistaken belief that the truths of religion have never changed.'[9]

The Polish Pope also had a huge ego. He was voted Man of the Year by *Time* magazine in January 1995. 'In these days of moral chaos, John Paul II is fiercely resolute about his ideas,' the magazine noted.

Not surprisingly, throughout his long period in office he favoured extending the scope of the fundamentalist doctrine of papal infallibility first formulated at Vatican I (1869–70). As pope, he had the world's biggest bully pulpit; when he spoke he expected the world to listen, and he demanded total assent and submission to all papal utterances.

> A token of the soaring cult of his personality: in his native Poland most churches now have on prominent show an outsize status of John Paul. As a Polish correspondent to the international Catholic weekly *The Tablet* noted at Christmas 2003: 'To my knowledge no other public figure has had so many statues erected in his life-time, except Joseph Stalin.'[10]

His role in the collapse of communism and the break-up of the Soviet Union is testimony to his political activism. In their book, Carl Bernstein (of Watergate fame) and Marco Politi claimed there was 'an informal secret alliance between the Holy See and the administration of President Ronald Reagan that would hasten the most profound political change of the age.'[11]

While the Vatican would never admit this, there is no doubt that after the Pope's visit to his native Poland in 1979, the CIA, with Reagan's blessing, would pass information and money to Wojtyła knowing that the Holy See intended to assist the Solidarity movement in its struggle against the Communist regime in Warsaw.

> In Washington, Reagan and Casey (the director of the CIA) had discussed the possibility of 'breaking Poland out of the Soviet orbit',

---

9   *The Times*, 3 August 1994.

10   Cornwell, *The Pope in Winter*, p. xvi.

11   Carl Bernstein and Marco Politi, *His Holiness: John Paul II and the Hidden History of Our Time* (London and New York: Doubleday, 1996), p. 11.

with help from the Holy Father. Solidarity and the Pope, as they saw it, were the levers with which Poland might begin to be pried loose. Wojtyła's accession to the papal throne and the ensuing events in Poland were redrawing the strategic map of the Cold War.[12]

However, the anti-Communist alliance between Rome and Washington would have very harmful effects in Central and South America. John Paul II was not just suspicious of but was hostile to one of the most important post-Vatican II developments – the emergence and growth of 'liberation theology'.

This nascent theology gained visibility at the Second General Conference of the Latin American Bishops, which took place in Medellín, Colombia, in the autumn of 1968. This conference undertook the application of the vision of Vatican II in the context of Latin America. It specifically endorsed a 'preferential opinion for the poor' and promoted a vision of the Church not only for the poor and with the poor, but a church of the poor (a vision, incidentally, which Pope Francis has made the cornerstone of his pontificate).

It was the Peruvian priest Gustavo Gutiérrez who, in his 1971 book *A Theology of Liberation* (English translation published in 1973), was the first to provide a systematic articulation of this new way of doing theology.

In addition to stressing a 'preferential option for the poor', it also sought to expand the traditional Catholic understanding of sin, which tends to be individualistic, to encompass 'social sin', which extends to social arrangements and socio-economic structures that create and perpetuate hunger and poverty.

However, where Gutiérrez and other advocates of liberation theology caused alarm in the Vatican was through their use of and reliance on a form of social analysis that drew on elements of Marxism and the class struggle. Gutiérrez had translated the Christian concept of 'salvation' into terms of 'liberation'. He had argued that the evil from which Latin America had to be freed was not just individual sin, but 'social sins' – injustice, oppression, deprivation, hunger and misery. The gospels, he said, should be reread from the point of view of the oppressed.

---

12   Ibid.

To Karol Wojtyła, with his experience of the Marxist regime in Poland, this was a bridge too far. He was still in his homeland in 1968 when the conference in Medellín took place, still archbishop of Kraków to which he had been appointed in 1963 by Paul VI, who made him a cardinal in 1967. But in January 1979, when he went to open the next meeting of CELAM in Puebla, Mexico, he was John Paul II (having been elected at the papal conclave of October 1978) and he went there with a very clear message.

The late Peter Hebblethwaite, who served for years as the Vatican affairs correspondent of the *National Catholic Reporter*, wrote: 'John Paul's address at Puebla was a clear rejection of some of the main theses of liberation theology.'

The Pope's words stunned the assembled bishops. 'In many of the Pope's public speeches, politics and religion are inseparably linked, despite his attempts to draw the biblical distinction between the spheres of Caesar and of God, and his criticism of priests who engage in political activities.' So wrote David Willey, the BBC's Rome correspondent in his 1993 book.[13] He went on to say that 'the first Slav ever to occupy Saint Peter's throne would inevitably become the most politically influential pope of modern times'.[14]

Willey had also stressed that many members of the Catholic Church had come to regard 'the Wojtyła pontificate as a bulldozer papacy, in which all internal opposition has been systematically flattened'.[15]

When Karol Wojtyła died on 2 April 2005 after a very long pontificate (twenty-six and a half years), the *Guardian*, two days later in its Comment and Analysis page, carried two contrasting assessments of his pontificate. In one, the historian Timothy Garton Ash described him as 'the greatest political actor of the last quarter-century', going on to explain that by this he meant 'a person who makes things happen in the world'.

The other article, by Terry Eagleton, professor of cultural theory at Manchester University, was blistering in its criticism of John Paul II. 'He was', Eagleton concluded, 'one of the greatest disasters for the Christian Church since Charles Darwin.' The author said the 'greatest crime of his

---

13   David Willey, *God's Politician: John Paul II and the Vatican* (London and Boston: Faber and Faber, 1993).

14   Ibid., p. xii.

15   Ibid., p. 233.

papacy' was neither his part in the cover-up of child sex abuse nor his 'neanderthal attitude' to women.

> It was the grotesque irony by which the Vatican condemned – as a 'culture of death' – condoms, which might have saved countless Catholics in the developing world from an agonising AIDS death. The Pope goes to his eternal reward with those deaths on his hands.[16]

---

16   *The Guardian,* 4 April 2005.

Chapter 15

GOD'S POLITICIANS:
LUTHER AND BONHOEFFER

Bonhoeffer's life and work
would have been political if the
Nazis had never existed.

Stanley Hauerwas

During the Second World War (1939–45) the town of Wittenberg was one of the few in Germany not bombed by the Allies. 'That exemption was a tribute to the worldwide impact of a monk-lecturer's spiritual turmoil in what in 1517 was one of Europe's newest universities.'[1]

The reference is to Martin Luther, an Augustinian priest who has gone down in history as the man who shattered the unity of Western Christendom. In the process he directly challenged the authority of the pope. 'For Luther and his colleagues the freedom from papal tyranny was only a beginning.'[2]

What Luther started came to be known as the Protestant Reformation. 'Politics and religion were, at this time, inextricably linked and with the Reformation the political face of Europe was irrevocably changed.'[3]

---

1   Diarmaid MacCulloch, *A History of Christianity* (London: Penguin Books, 2009), p. 605.

2   Andrew Pettegree, *Brand Luther: 1517, Printing, and the Making of the Reformation* (New York: Penguin Books, 2015), p. 323.

3   Vivian HH Green, *Luther and the Reformation* (London: New English Library, 1974).

The act that has traditionally been regarded as marking the beginning of the Reformation over five hundred years ago may never have occurred. Some scholars doubt that Luther actually nailed his list of 95 theses to the door of the church in Wittenberg (though MacCulloch thinks it probably did happen), but they were sent to the local archbishop, and then through him to Rome. Their effect was dramatic, turning an unheralded monk into the most famous man in Europe.

'Few people had heard of Martin Luther before he posted his 95 theses to the door of the castle church at Wittenberg on 31 October 1517; but within less than four years he had become a familiar and feared name in the universities and courts of every European country.'[4] What is not in doubt is that the posting of the theses marked what another Luther scholar has called 'one of the seminal moments in Western civilisation.'[5]

Luther left a lasting and complex legacy, but one facet of it – anchored in his political philosophy – was to have dire consequences for the Lutheran Church in Germany following the rise to power of Adolf Hitler and the Nazis in 1933. This posed daunting challenges for all the Christian churches, but the challenge for Lutherans was especially acute due to Luther's teaching, especially his interpretation of Paul's Epistle to the Romans 13:1: 'Let every soul be subject to the higher powers. For there is no power but of God: the powers that be are ordained of God.'

This, an unqualified instruction to 'Obey Caesar' – or, four hundred years later, 'Obey Hitler' – has led some commentators to stress that there was a dark side to Luther's legacy. The new ideas spread by him inspired the Peasants' War of 1524–5; this was a big test for Luther because the peasants who revolted had thought they were putting some of his theories into practice. Disillusionment and unhappiness had been brewing among Germany's poor, and this boiled over. 'Luther was forced to choose sides, and threw his lot in with those princes who had embraced his Protestantism,' says Peter Stanford. In other words, Luther turned against the peasants and sided with the powerful.[6]

This was a problem that would have implications down to the present day because Luther, for all his revolutionary zeal, thought Christians

---

4   Ibid., p. 9.

5   Pettegree, *Brand Luther*, p. ix.

6   Peter Stanford, *Martin Luther: Catholic Dissident* (London: Hodder and Stoughton, 2017), p. 310.

should obey authority, even if it was foolish or evil. He, therefore, urged the princes to take harsh measures against the peasants to ensure their defeat. Their revolt has been described as 'Europe's most massive and widespread popular uprising before the 1789 French Revolution'.[7]

Luther's support for the authorities against the peasants was not a matter of self-preservation, however. His application of the doctrine of the 'two kingdoms' – leaving to the State earthly matters, and to the Church spiritual matters – came to be seen as a cruel betrayal by the rebellious peasants who had placed their faith and hopes in him as their saviour.

Augustine's *City of God* – in which the great Bishop of Hippo outlined the existence of two spheres, an earthly city and the 'city' of God – served as the foundation of Luther's model of 'two kingdoms', but his interpretation of a key passage (13:1) in Paul's Epistle to the Romans was to have catastrophic repercussions four hundred years later in Nazi Germany.

William L. Shirer has described Luther as 'a ferocious believer in absolute obedience to political authority'.[8] Did the essence of Luther's theme of obedience to superior powers (civil powers) contain, as one commentator has claimed, the seeds of the proto-Hitlerite stance that came to fruition in the wake of the rise of Adolf Hitler in Germany in the 1930s, emasculating mainstream Lutheranism when confronted by the burgeoning evil of the Nazi State?[9]

William Temple, who was the Anglican archbishop of York (1929–42), and of Canterbury (1942–4), was in no doubt. Rejecting the Lutheran doctrine on the spheres of Church and State, he said: 'It is easy to see how Luther prepared the way for Hitler'.[10]

It was left to the Confessional Church (set up in opposition to the Nazified Reich Church) and to three of its pastors, Karl Barth, Martin Niemöller and Dietrich Bonhoeffer in particular, to attempt to free the Lutheran Church from the domination of the State and allow it to bear independent witness in the face of Nazi tyranny.

---

7   Diarmaid MacCulloch, *The Reformation: A History* (London: Penguin Books, 2003), p. 158.

8   William L. Shirer, *The Rise and Fall of the Third Reich* (London: Pan Books, 1969), p. 294.

9   Ian Thomson, *The Observer*, 26 June 2016.

10   Alan Wilkinson, *Christian Socialism: Scott Holland to Tony Blair* (London: SCM Press, 1998), p. 119.

Barth vigorously repudiated the Lutheran model of a church subordinate to the civil authorities. His conception of the relations that should obtain between Church and State was closer to the Calvinist model that allowed the people to resist tyrannical governments because the people's covenant was with governments whose authority did not supersede the people's covenant with God.

The Lutheran Church's dependence upon the State 'moulded its history for the next four centuries and even in the twentieth century did much to condition its readiness with which it accepted the religious policy of Hitler and his associates'.[11]

The influence of Luther had a fossilising effect on the Lutheran tradition in Germany during the critical period 1933–45 following the collapse of the Weimar Republic (1919–33).

> Resistance by Protestant churchmen was handicapped by a four-hundred-year-old tradition of 'throne and altar' based on Roman chapter 13, with its functional separation of temporal and spiritual powers, and by the political homelessness of German Protestants during the Weimar Republic, a problem many resolved by supporting the Nazi Party.[12]

In a 1983 article on Martin Luther headed 'The Strange Paradox', Neal Ascherson said that Luther's

> disastrous insistence that all State power – even a satanically evil government – is sent by God and must be obeyed was almost to annihilate the moral authority of German Lutherans where they bowed down to Hitler. Only the tiny nucleus of the 'Confessing Church,' with Bonhoeffer and Niemöller, found their way out of the dilemma and resisted.[13]

---

11 Green, *Luther and the Reformation*, p. 204.

12 Michael Burleigh, *The Third Reich: A New History* (London: Pan Books, 2001), p. 721.

13 *The Observer*, 17 November 1983.

To free the Church from the domination of the State was one of the main aims of the Confessing Church (so-called because its adherents believed they were 'confessing' true Christian doctrine). This was highlighted in a key document – the Barmen Declaration of 1934. This emerged from the first Synod of the Confessing Church held in the town of Barmen in Germany which defined the beliefs and mission of the Church in the face of the Nazis. The text was largely the work of Karl Barth, and was signed by Bonhoeffer.

'The post-Reformation practice of Church–State relations resulted in the Church becoming a virtual department of State.'[14] While this was a problem, it was what Hitler wanted and how he saw matters in 1933 – a Nazified Church that would do his bidding and be supportive of the Third Reich.

It was left to the tiny Confessing Church to challenge this, to bear witness to the gospel of Jesus Christ, to show their fellow Germans that they had a duty to reject the subordination of the Church to the State.

Bonhoeffer was born in Breslau in 1906. He was ordained in November 1931 at the age of twenty-five. Early in his life he decided he wanted to be a pastor and a theologian, and he was to become influenced by the great Swiss theologian, Karl Barth (1886–1968), who taught in several German universities between 1921 and 1935 before returning to Switzerland where he spent the rest of his life.

> Barth and Bonhoeffer were in close contact with one another in the late 1920s and early 1930s, as Germany attempted to recover from one war and began to mobilise for another. They shared intense mutual concern for the relationship of German Christianity to the changing German State. When Hitler became Reich Chancellor in 1933, this relationship changed dramatically.[15]

The Vatican, in a shameful episode that left many of Germany's twenty-three million Catholics (and their bishops who hadn't been consulted) feeling betrayed, negotiated a concordat with Hitler. The concordat was signed on

---

14   John A. Moses, *The Reluctant Revolutionary: Dietrich Bonhoeffer's Collision with Prusso-German History* (New York and Oxford: Berghahn Books, 2009), p. 7.

15   Elizabeth Phillips, *Political Theology* (London: T&T Clark International, 2012), p. 64.

20 July 1933, less than six months after Hitler became chancellor. At the time the Catholic Centre Party was one of the leading parties in the Reichstag.

'Hitler wanted a concordat for two principal reasons: Firstly, for prestige, to make his upstart regime appear more respectable abroad; secondly, to obtain control over, if not to eliminate, the refractory Centre Party,' according to Anthony Rhodes.[16] The Vatican did his dirty work for him – as part of the new deal with Hitler the Centre Party was disowned by Rome and instructed to stand down. An important source of opposition to Nazism had been neutralised.

With the signing of the concordat, the Nazi State had gained vital recognition. 'Within six months of its birth, the Third Reich had been given full approval by the highest spiritual power on earth.'[17]

Now the Führer could turn his attention to the Protestant churches. The problem was that the forty-five million German Protestants were represented by twenty-eight (mainly Lutheran) churches. Germany in 1933 was over 95 per cent Christian.

Hitler wanted a totally subservient and united Reich Church under a Reich bishop. The man chosen was Pastor Müller, a notorious Nazi sympathiser. Those Protestants who favoured a Nazified national church called themselves 'German Christians', and at a synod in Wittenberg, where Luther had first defied the pope, they elected Müller as their leader. Although resolutions were passed demanding 'One People, One Reich, One Faith', the new Reich bishop was unable to unify Protestants.

Those who opposed Nazi control of the churches decided to break away and form a new grouping of Christians; Bonhoeffer became one of the leading members.

Today there is a statue of Bonhoeffer in the heart of London. It is one of ten modern martyrs, unveiled in July 1998, which stand above the west entrance to Westminster Abbey. Dr Martin Luther King, Archbishop Óscar Romero and Fr Maximilian Kolbe are also honoured there. Bonhoeffer was hanged in Flossenbürg concentration camp on 9 April 1945. He had been accused of involvement in a plot to assassinate Hitler. He has no known grave, but his legacy endures.

---

16   Anthony Rhodes, *The Vatican in the Age of the Dictators (1922–1945)* (New York: Holt, Rinehart and Winston, 1973), p. 173.

17   Ibid., p. 177.

'There is no doubt that Bonhoeffer's lifework has captured the imagination of a considerable number of Christians of most traditions throughout the world,' says John A. Moses.[18]

> His was a life that was at once theological and political. It was so, however, not because he died at the hands of the Nazis. Bonhoeffer's life and work would have been political if the Nazis had never existed; for Bonhoeffer saw clearly that the failure of the Church when confronted with Hitler began long before the Nazi challenge. Hitler forced a Church long accustomed to privileges dependent on its invisibility to become visible. The Church in Germany, however, had simply lost the resources to reclaim its space in the world. How that space can be reclaimed, not only in the face of the Nazis but when times seem 'normal', is the heart of Bonhoeffer's theological politics.[19]

Another facet of Luther's dark legacy was his fierce antisemitism. This was expressed most notably in his most notorious work, *On the Jews and Their Lies* (1543). In it, his advice to the German princes was uncompromising. 'The Jewish presence in Germany was a plague that should be eradicated; synagogues should be destroyed and Jewish books confiscated. None should suggest that the Jews were indispensable for financial reasons; now was the time to remove them from Germany.' That's how Pettegree sums up the violent tone of the message. And he goes on: 'Of all of Luther's writings none was more damaging to his later reputation, particularly in modern times, after these passages had been cited with such enthusiasm by the ideologues of National Socialism.'[20]

Luther had, in effect, injected a poison into the bloodstream of German Christianity that would culminate in the Holocaust during the Third Reich under Hitler. 'He said some terrible things about Jews,' according to Nick Baines, the Anglican bishop of Leeds, 'which in turn had terrible consequences four centuries later'.[21]

---

18   Moses, *The Reluctant Revolutionary*, p. 250.

19   Stanley Hauerwas, 'Dietrich Bonhoeffer' in Peter Scott and William T. Cavanaugh, eds, *The Blackwell Companion to Political Theology* (Oxford: Blackwell, 2004), p. 139.

20   Pettegree, *Brand Luther*, p. 297.

21   *The Observer*, 30 October 2016.

Chapter 16

GOD'S POLITICIANS:
DAY AND THATCHER

There is no such thing as society.

Margaret Thatcher

On 24 September 2015, in a historic address to the US Congress, Pope Francis mentioned four iconic Americans he found particularly inspiring – Abraham Lincoln, Martin Luther King, Dorothy Day and Thomas Merton. Francis, who was making history by being the first pope ever to address a joint sitting of Congress, said the following:

> A nation can be considered great when it defends liberty as Lincoln did; when it fosters a culture which enables people to 'dream' of full rights for all their brothers and sisters as Martin Luther King sought to do; when it strives for justice and the cause of the oppressed as Dorothy Day did by her tireless work; the fruit of a faith which becomes dialogue and sows peace in the contemplative style of Thomas Merton.

The inclusion of Dorothy Day probably surprised many who watched the televised address. Not a whole lot was known about her in mainstream

Catholic circles; she was just known for being meddlesome and troublesome. Social justice was never given much priority in American political or socio-economic circles. It carried with it left-wing connotations, and that made it anathema in a society where antipathy to communism and socialism was deep-rooted. That this antipathy also existed at the highest levels of her own church made her inclusion by the Pope all the more baffling in some quarters.

There would be neither surprise nor bafflement, however, among those who were aware of Pope Francis's desire for a church 'that is poor and for the poor', and that he would see in Dorothy Day's commitment to helping the poor and oppressed in society a shining example of Christian living.

The entry for Day in the *Oxford Dictionary of the Christian Church* offers a concise pen picture:

> Day, Dorothy (1897–1980), co-founder, with the visionary Frenchman Peter Maurin (1877–1949) of the lay-dominated Catholic Worker Movement in the USA. A radical socialist, she was involved in various disastrous personal relationships, but after the birth of a daughter, she became a Roman Catholic in 1927. In 1933, at the instigation of Maurin, she founded a monthly newspaper, *The Catholic Worker*, which made many American Roman Catholics conscious of the social teaching of Leo XIII in *Rerum novarum*; at its height it had a circulation of over one hundred thousand. She and Maurin also set up 'Houses of Hospitality' which provided food and shelter for needy men and women in New York and other cities during the Depression. In the 1940s and later, her pacifism caused divisions, but Catholic Worker communities still embrace voluntary poverty and provide hospitality for the homeless, exiled, and forsaken. Day fostered Catholic Worker retreats which stressed the need for mortification.[1]

Though not particularly religious in her youth (her parents were not churchgoers), she started to read the Bible in her teens, and therein she found a religious foundation for her natural sympathy for the downtrodden

---

1 EA Livingstone, ed., *The Concise Oxford Dictionary of the Christian Church* (Oxford: Oxford University Press, 2006), p. 162.

and society's outcasts. At eighteen she got a job as a reporter on the *Call*, a small socialist paper in New York. This was in 1917 as the United States was about to enter World War I. The roots of her pacifism can be traced to this period; she was opposed to war 'on the grounds that it was a capitalist device'. It was also during this period that she interviewed Leon Trotsky, who was working in New York for the Russian paper *Novy Mir* and not yet an international figure, though he soon would be.

On 27 December 1927, Day took a life-changing step by getting the ferry to Staten Island where she was baptised in the local Catholic Church there. She was twenty-eight years old. She would later talk of 'my background of socialism and communism and my conversion to Catholicism'.

In a biographical article in 2019, Robert McNamara filled in some of the background: 'At the time of her conversion, she was an unmarried mother with a complicated past that included life as a bohemian writer in Greenwich Village, unhappy love affairs, and an abortion that rendered her emotionally devastated.'[2] During this period also she had a platonic relationship with the playwright Eugene O'Neill.

Her chance meeting with Peter Maurin (which she would regard as 'providential') would have profound implications for her future life. He was born in 1877 in the province of Languedoc in France; later, the sight of poverty in the slums of Paris and exposure to the anarchic writings of Peter Kropotkin would radicalise him. In New York he went looking for Day after reading some of her articles on social justice. Their meeting would lead to the foundation of the Catholic Worker Movement – a movement that combined pacifism with direct aid for the poor, the indigent and the homeless with non-violent direct action – including civil disobedience – on their behalf.

The Catholic Worker newspaper was launched by Day and Maurin on 1 May 1933 to make Catholics *more* aware of Church teaching on social justice. Published from New York seven times a year, it sold for one penny. Its advocacy of radical solutions to poverty and homelessness placed it outside the mainstream of American Catholicism. 'While she hated every kind of tyranny and never ceased to be thankful for America having taken in so many people fleeing poverty and repression, she was fierce in her criticism of

---

2   Robert McNamara, 'Biography of Dorothy Day, Founder of the Catholic Worker Movement', *ThoughtCo*, https://www.thoughtco.com/dorothy-day-biography-4154465 (accessed April 2022).

capitalism and consumerism,' wrote Jim Forest in 1998. 'She said America had a tendency to treat people like Kleenex; use them, and throw them away. Our problems stem, she said, from our acceptance of this filthy, rotten system.'[3] A column by Dorothy in that very first issue contained this passage:

> For those who think there is no hope for the future, no recognition of their plight – this little paper is addressed. It is printed to call their attention to the fact that the Catholic Church has a social programme – to let them know there are men of God who are working not only for their spiritual, but for their material welfare.

Within a few years the circulation exceeded one hundred thousand.

> The Catholic Worker has been a small but very significant movement within Catholicism since its beginning in 1933. The movement in theory and in practice has espoused a radical type of social ethics based on the gospel … There have been other instances of radical Catholicism in the United States, but none has rivalled the importance of the Catholic Worker Movement begun by Peter Maurin and Dorothy Day in 1933.[4]

Day was a very passionate, committed woman, a woman of great courage and determination, who was prepared to risk imprisonment in the cause of justice.

> During the period that Cardinal Spellman tried to steer Catholics in the New York diocese to conservative causes, Dorothy Day founded the Catholic Worker Movement to promote progressive policies on poverty, labour, social justice, civil liberties, and international disarmament.[5]

---

3   Jim Forrest, 'Dorothy Day – Saint and Troublemaker', Catholic Education Resource Centre, www.catholiceducation.org/en/culture/catholic-contributions/dorothy-day-saint-and-troublemaker. html (accessed April 2022).

4   Charles E. Curran, *American Catholic Social Ethics* (Notre Dame and London: University of Notre Dame Press, 1982), p. 130.

5   Kenneth D. Wald and Allison Calhoun-Brown, *Religion and Politics in the United States* (New York and Oxford: Rowman and Littlefield Publishers, 2007) (5th edn), p. 252.

Having publicly criticised former first lady Eleanor Roosevelt (he saw her as a 'flaccid liberal who let emotions obscure reason'; he was convinced she was a 'Communist dupe'), Cardinal Spellman – who hated labour unions – moved to break a strike by poorly paid gravediggers (members of the United Cemetery Workers' Union) at Calvary Cemetery in the borough of Queens in New York in March 1949, using seminarians as scabs. Dorothy Day was one of the few to protest. The Cardinal's biographer had this to say: 'Dorothy Day was one of the few who supported the union. She and some of her staff from the *Catholic Worker* passed out leaflets in front of the Cardinal's residence and were arrested. The police forbade the gravediggers to picket Spellman's house'.[6]

On war, especially the Vietnam War, the contrast between Spellman and Day couldn't be sharper. For her, war was 'simply murder wrapped in flags'. Spellman, on the other hand, was one of the most outspoken supporters of the US involvement in Vietnam. 'The Cardinal became one of the most hawkish, arguably the most hawkish, leaders in the United States,' according to his biographer. 'By 1965 he clashed with the Pope, who desperately tried to bring peace in Vietnam as Spellman pounded the drums of war'.[7]

Given Cardinal Spellman's fierce anti-liberalism in the Archdiocese of New York and beyond, it seemed strange that he never confronted Day, though she never sought official approval for her work and never asked for episcopal endorsement. John Cooney, in his acclaimed biography of the Cardinal, offers an explanation.

> In the light of the archbishop's attacks against liberals, his priests were confused when Spellman failed to move against Dorothy Day and her radical worker movement, which was based in New York. Her newspaper, the *Catholic Worker*, addressed problems of race, labour, housing and hunger, and her solutions ran counter to Spellman's conservative philosophy. The archbishop believed the Church's duty to the less fortunate ended with raising

---

6   John Cooney, *The American Pope: The Life and Times of Francis Cardinal Spellman* (New York: Times Books, 1984).

7   Ibid., p. 245.

funds for charitable institutions. She believed in changing society itself to help those who needed it, and she became a heroine to young Catholics in a later age.

Spellman, however, wasn't a man who looked for trouble. He shrewdly realised that censuring Dorothy Day would create more problems than it would solve. Though her newspaper had a circulation of 150,000, the number of people active in her movement was small; their numbers and influence might increase if he focused more attention on her. Moreover, such a move wouldn't be popular in the Church ... She was a reminder of what many priests had once intended doing with their lives. When asked why he didn't silence her, Spellman appeared momentarily startled. 'She might be a saint,' he replied.[8]

Dorothy Day remained active until her death on 29 November 1980, in her room at a Catholic Worker residence in New York. She was buried on Staten Island, near the site of her conversion. She was eighty-three. The funeral was on 2 December at the Nativity Catholic Church. William D. Miller described what happened:

At the church door, Cardinal Terence Cooke met the body to bless it. As the procession stopped for this rite, a demented person pushed his way through the crowd and bending low over the coffin peered at it intently. No one interfered, because, as even the funeral directors understood, it was in such as this man that Dorothy had seen the face of God.[9]

Today there are those who believe it is only a matter of time before she is canonised. With regard to her legacy, Miller says: 'It was nothing material, for the New York archdiocese felt it appropriate to pay for the opening of her grave. Her legacy was a vision – a vision of ending time with its evil nightmares by bringing Christ back on Earth.'[10]

---

8 Ibid., p. 90.

9 William D. Miller, *Dorothy Day: A Biography* (San Francisco: Harper and Row, 1982), p. 517.

10 Ibid., p. 518.

Unlike Dorothy Day, Margaret Thatcher was born into a staunchly religious household, and religion would feature throughout her life. Her father was a lay Methodist preacher and she would follow in his footsteps. As her biographer John Campbell pointed out: 'Mrs Thatcher was a preacher before she was a politician.'[11]

In her memoir Thatcher describes how, having won the 1979 general election, during the drive from Buckingham Palace to No. 10, she rehearsed what she was going to say to the assembled media in front of the most famous front door in the world. 'I quoted a famous prayer attributed to St Francis of Assisi, beginning, "Where there is discord, may we bring harmony".'[12] This was not something done on a whim; it was quite deliberate and planned. It said a lot about the woman who had just become Britain's first female leader.

> In 1979, unbeknownst to most of the public at the time, Britain had elected its most religious prime minister since William Gladstone, one who from the very first moment of her premiership referenced her spiritual motivation by reciting a prayer on the steps of No. 10. Margaret Thatcher, though, did not simply draw on Christianity for rhetorical ornamentation for, as the daughter of a Methodist lay-preacher, she had a clear understanding of the religious basis of her political values.[13]

This is how Eliza Filby supplied a context for what was a defining moment. In her book, she explained the background: 'Before the 1979 result had been confirmed, Thatcher had asked her chief speechwriter and dramatist Ronald Miller to prepare something for her to say outside No 10. When Miller informed her of his idea for a prayer, Margaret wept.'[14]

Margaret Thatcher had been first elected MP for Finchley in 1959, but earlier in the 1950s she moved away from Methodism and became an Anglican. Political expediency played a part in that decision – in the 1950s Conservatives were still expected to be Anglicans, and the politically

---

11   John Campbell, *Margaret Thatcher: The Grocer's Daughter* (London: Jonathan Cape, 2000), p. 48.

12   Margaret Thatcher, *The Downing Street Years* (London: HarperCollins, 1993), p. 19.

13   Eliza Filby, *God and Mrs Thatcher* (London: Biteback Publishing, 2015), p. xvii.

14   Ibid., p. 117.

ambitious young woman from Grantham didn't want her non-conformist past becoming an obstacle to advancement. But the influence of John Wesley didn't wane, and, as prime minister, the 'Iron Lady' would clash with the leadership of the Church of England.

This was especially so in December 1985 when a commission headed by Robert Runcie, archbishop of Canterbury, issued a report, *Faith in the City: A Call for Action by Church and Nation.*

> It chastised both the Church of England for its failures to do more to sustain blighted urban areas, and the hardline conservative government of Margaret Thatcher for its free-market economic reforms and their social impact … The Prime Minister declared herself 'absolutely shocked' by its findings.[15]

In the words of Filby, *Faith in the City* 'would prove to be one of the most incisive critiques of Thatcher's Britain. It laid bare, in stark and shocking terms the "two nations" that existed in Britain'.[16] Its recommendations were labelled by one anonymous cabinet member as 'Marxist'.

The report was, as Filby emphasised, 'important in fuelling the growing public perception of Thatcherism as a doctrine that entirely prioritised profit over human needs; a view that particularly rankled Margaret Thatcher'.[17]

This didn't in any way inhibit Margaret Thatcher. She had very clear thoughts about the role of Christianity and its relationship with the political sphere. In 1987 she had uttered words that her critics would pounce on: 'There is no such thing as society'.[18] In its place her religo-political values would promote an individualism that, once she became prime minister, would bring her into conflict with the Church of England.

In an address to the General Assembly of the Church of Scotland in 1988, she left no doubt about Christianity's role: 'Christianity is about spiritual redemption, not social reform.'

---

15   Peter Stanford, *If These Stones Could Talk: The History of Christianity in Britain and Ireland through Twenty Buildings* (London: Hodder and Stoughton, 2021), p. 342.

16   Filby, *God and Mrs Thatcher*, p. 172.

17   Ibid., p. 175.

18   Interview for *Woman's Own*, 23 September 1987.

Jonathan Raban of the *Observer* responded to this speech with a stinging critique published in the form of a short book. It brought her audience back, he said, to 'a soundly fundamentalist view of man' while also relaunching the attack on 'mediating institutions' – in other words, there would be no room for cooperatives, unions or other manifestations of solidarity, and even the State itself would have a very limited role in providing for the needs of the poor, the unemployed and the marginalised. Thatcher's speech was permeated, Raban said, by an 'eccentric theology'. It was 'stamped throughout with her ... scornful and impatient certitude'. He said it was an 'audacious' piece of work.[19] 'Thatcherism may have laid the foundations for a culture in which individualism and self-reliance could thrive, but, ultimately, it created a culture in which only selfishness and excess were rewarded.'[20]

Hugo Young said the same thing in a slightly different way when he pointed out that the brand of conservatism that flourished under Thatcher 'gave too much emphasis to individualism and not enough to the collective obligations of society'. Of Thatcher, he also said: 'She thought about religious questions more than most prime ministers have publicly admitted doing', yet her view of religion was distinctly 'other-worldly'. As she told her Church of Scotland audience, she 'always had difficulty with interpreting the biblical precept to love our neighbours "as ourselves"'. The problem all along was that Thatcher had a very narrow understanding of what constituted society.[21]

In essence, Thatcher saw society as a collection of atomised individuals. Despite her strict upbringing as a Methodist and her time as a lay preacher, she found nothing in the Bible to justify a socio-political dimension to Christianity. The contrast with Dorothy Day could hardly be sharper – the latter believed passionately in mutual aid rooted in an ethic of caring and sharing, and, in so doing, defied the materialism of modern society in the name of a literal Christianity. She saw her Christian mission as an attempt to live a Christ-like life among the poor, the exploited, the downtrodden, the voiceless, the marginalised and the dispossessed.

19   Jonathan Raban, *God, Man and Mrs Thatcher* (London: Chatto & Windus, 1989), p. 67.

20   Filby, *God and Mrs Thatcher*, p. 347.

21   Hugo Young, *One of Us: A Biography of Margaret Thatcher* (London: Pan Books, 1990), pp. 417–18.

Chapter 17

ISLAM: A FAITH TO BE FEARED?

The reform of Islam is shaping up
to be the most important issue in political
ideology of the twenty-first century.

Steven Pinker

In August 2007 the *Irish Times* devoted most of its Opinion & Analysis page to the debate: 'Does Islam encourage terrorism?' The 'Yes' side of the argument was put by Susan Philips, a political analyst and author of *The London Bombings*. The 'No' side was put by Syyed Siraj H. Zaidi, an actor, TV producer and a founding member of the Three Faiths Forum of Ireland which brings together Muslims, Jews and Christians. According to Philips:

> Many consider Islam to contain peaceful approaches, but within its literature, significant space exists to nurture a radical vanguard force, which is religiously driven and committed to world domination through a process of jihad. Unless Islam is understood in such terms and is held in check by world opinion, the power of Western institutions or moderate Islamic elites, it will continue unchecked in its quest to establish a global caliphate.

In an earlier reference to the 9/11 attacks in the USA and the July 2005 London bombings, she said the men responsible

> had a deep religious conviction that they were carrying out their Qur'anic duty to extend the kingdom of Islam worldwide. No matter what moderates argue, countless suicide attacks by jihadis against the Western infidel, as well as against fellow Muslims whose interpretations of their faith seem to vary from their own, are given a religious justification.

Syyed Siraj H. Zaidi, on the other hand, dismissed the question he was asked to address as 'absurd' as it showed a profound lack of knowledge of Islam. Islam, as described in the Qur'an, he said, 'is a modern, enlightened, progressive religion.'[1]

> One cannot even juxtapose the word terrorism with Islam – they are contradictory terms. In true Islam, terror does not exist. In Islam, killing a human is an act equal in gravity to unbelief. Islam, like all monotheist religions, is a religion of peace and tolerance. If one looks into the history of Islam, one would find that this most sublime religion became the victim of extreme brutality and terrorism by so-called Muslims who did not follow the Prophet's instructions and teaching of Qur'an, immediately after his demise.

What, then, is 'true' Islam? It is difficult to square the assertion that Islam is a 'religion of peace and tolerance' with Wahhabism – the version of Islam that is the official, State religion of Saudi Arabia, or with that propagated by Sayyid Qutb, the Egyptian writer described as 'a leading theorist of violent jihad'. We know that the nineteen hijackers responsible for the 9/11 attacks (fifteen of whom came from Saudi Arabia) were disciples of Osama bin Laden, whose 'militant brand of Islam was deeply influenced by Sayyid Qutb', according to Karen Armstrong.[2]

---

1   Opinion & Analysis, *The Irish Times*, 13 August 2007.

2   Karen Armstrong, *Islam: A Short History* (London: Phoenix, 2002), p. 159.

The idea of Islam as a modern, enlightened, progressive religion is also difficult to square with the fanatical response from Pakistani Islamic extremists who, in November 2018, demonstrated in the streets, demanding the death penalty for Asia Bibi, the Christian woman who spent eight years on death row in Pakistan for blasphemy before her acquittal by the country's Supreme Court in January 2019. In dismissing the case against her, the Chief Justice Asif Saeed Khosa said: 'The image of Islam we are showing to the world gives me much grief and sorrow.'[3] While still in prison, members of Asia Bibi's family were 'hunted by extremists going house to house with photographs to try to track them down.'[4] Angry mobs carrying placards saying 'Hang Asia' caused considerable disruption. After her acquittal she was offered asylum in Canada.

Then there was the gruesome murder at a remote campsite at the foot of the Atlas Mountains in Morocco of two young female Scandinavian backpackers in December 2018 by fanatics shouting 'enemies of God' and 'It's Allah's will' and pledging their allegiance to Isis leader Abu Bakr al-Baghdadi.[5] This was just the latest in a series of atrocities committed by people claiming an alliance with Isis. One could insist that the latter is an aberration, and not representative of 'true' Islam, but the fact remains that its members and supporters claim to find justification for their murderous actions in the Qur'an.

What is a scholar of religion, particularly of Islam, to make of a report from Tehran that appeared in an Irish newspaper in 2010? These were the opening paragraphs:

> An Iranian newspaper said yesterday that Carla Bruni, the wife of France's president, Nicolas Sarkozy, deserved to die after she expressed solidarity with a woman sentenced to be stoned for adultery.
>
> The hardline daily Kayhan called Bruni a 'prostitute' whose lifestyle meant she deserved a similar fate as the Iranian woman sentenced to death for adultery.[6]

---

3   *Daily Telegraph*, 30 January 2019.

4   *The Guardian*, 27 November 2018.

5   *The Irish Sun*, 21 December 2018.

6   *Irish Examiner*, 1 September 2010.

In a speech to the Bloomberg organisation in London on 23 April 2014, the former British prime minister Tony Blair warned that Islamic extremism represented the biggest threat to global security. He said radical Islam was an extremist ideology whose adherents were prepared to kill a large number of people because of their beliefs. A month later he expanded on this in a feature article.

> What is that ideology? Let me state some things very clearly. This ideology does not represent Islam. The majority of Muslims do not agree with it. They are repulsed by it. What might loosely be called Islamism is based on a politicisation of religion that is fundamentally incompatible with the modern world, for it assumes that there is one true religion, only one interpretation of that religion, and that this interpretation should prevail and dominate all countries' politics, government institutions, and social life. Those who do not share this view must be overcome.
>
> This Islamist ideology is a spectrum. At one extreme are groups such as Boko Haram. Other groups may not advocate violence but still preach a view of the world that is dangerous and hostile to those who disagree – for example the Muslim Brotherhood's statement in 2013 denouncing the UN women's declaration for, among other things, defending women's right to travel or work without their husband's permission.
>
> An Islamic ideology that mixes politics and religion in such a deadly way must be confronted. It is the ideology, not just the acts of extremism, that must be confronted.[7]

Much later, the historian Niall Ferguson lamented the West's failure to do this.

> Ask yourself how effectively we in the West have responded to the rise of militant Islam since the Iranian Revolution unleashed its Shi'ite variant and since 9/11 revealed the even more aggressive character of Sunni Islamism. I fear we have done no better than

---

7   *Irish Examiner*, 28 May 2014.

our grandfathers did ... A century ago it was the West's great blunder to think it would not matter if Lenin and his confederates took over the Russian Empire, despite their stated intention to plot world revolution and overthrow both democracy and capitalism. Incredible as it may seem, I believe we are capable of repeating that catastrophic error. I fear that, one day, we shall wake up to discover that the Islamists have repeated the Bolshevik achievement, which was to acquire the resources and capability to threaten our existence.[8]

It is interesting to note that another former British prime minister David Cameron gave voice to concerns similar to those on which Tony Blair focused. In a speech in Birmingham in July 2015 (while he was still prime minister), he said those who stir up antipathy to the West in response to perceived historic injustices or involvement in Middle East wars must be confronted.

We face a radical ideology that is not just subversive, but can seem exciting, that has often sucked people in from non-violence to violence, that is overpowering moderate voices within the debate and can gain traction because of issues of identity and failures of integration.

In a comment on Cameron's remarks, columnist Philip Johnston warned about the dangers of alienation of young Muslim men – and, increasingly, women – from the mainstream of society in the West.

It is their separation from the mainstream rather than the ideology itself that is the problem. Essentially, this has a lot to do with a shared religion, which is why those who say Islam is not the issue miss the point: it is not that its teachings are necessarily at fault, but Islam provides an impenetrable ethical and cultural carapace that repels liberal ideas. Add in the supposed 'glamour' offered by

---

8   *The Sunday Times*, 12 November 2017.

organisations like Isil and the misplaced sense of injustice that is continually invoked by Muslim spokesmen and you have a toxic cocktail that may manifest itself in violence.[9]

In his 2004 book *The War for Muslim Minds*, Gilles Kepel, professor at the Institute for Political Studies in Paris, had addressed these very concerns.

The most important battle in the war for Muslim minds during the next decade will be fought not in Palestine or Iraq but in these communities of believers on the outskirts of London, Paris, and other European cities, where Islam is already a growing part of the West. If European societies are able to integrate these Muslim populations, handicapped as they are by dispossession, and steer them towards prosperity, this new generation of Muslims may become the Islamic vanguard of the next decade, offering their co-religionists a new vision of the faith and a way out of the dead-end politics that has paralysed their countries of origin.[10]

Professor Kepel was writing that in 2004 – but how much has changed since, and has the change been for better or worse? Sixteen years after his book appeared, a report from Paris, where he was based, left little doubt that change in the interim was very much for the worse. These were the first three paragraphs of Lara Marlowe's report:

'We must attack separatist Islam,' French president Emmanuel Macron said yesterday in a long-awaited speech on France's relations with its Muslim minority.

Macron defined separatist Islam as 'a conscious, theorised, politico-religious project which is at odds with the values of the Republic'. He said it leads to a 'counter society' in which children are removed from school, while sports and cultural activities are exploited as sectarian vehicles of indoctrination.

---

9   *The Daily Telegraph*, 21 July 2015.

10   Gilles Kepel, *The War for Muslim Minds: Islam and the West* (Cambridge and London: Harvard University Press, 2004), pp. 8–9.

The ultimate goal of 'separatist Islam' was 'to take control of society,' Macron said.[11]

In light of the above, the key question remains – can Islam, and especially its extremist strands, be reconciled with modernity and modern society, which cherishes democracy, gender equality, religious freedom, pluralism and freedom of expression? Can extremist Muslims be successfully integrated into liberal society?

A further, and major, complication, stems from the Sunni–Shia divide within Islam itself. 'The 1,400-year-old schism between Sunni and Shia Muslims has rarely been as toxic as it is today, feeding wars and communal strife in Syria, Iraq, Yemen, Pakistan, Afghanistan and elsewhere,' according to John McHugo, a historian and international lawyer whose books include *A Concise History of Sunnis and Shi'is.*

> But what lies behind the Sunni–Shia split? All Muslims agree on the text of the Qur'an as the word of God – but they also ask who is to trust as the transmitters of Muhammad's custom or *sunna*, which is vital to the practice of their faith. The divide between Muslims may go back to the lifetime of the Prophet, or at least to his final hours.[12]

The Sunni–Shia split is really about succession. Who should be the caliph after Muhammad's death? 'The term caliph comes from the Arabic word for successor – variously interpreted as successor to the messenger of God or successor chosen by God,' explained Giles Fraser in a 2016 article. 'Sunni Muslims believe the caliph should be elected, Shia Muslims that he should be a biological descendent of the Prophet Muhammad.'[13] This divide over succession would, over time, have terrible, bloody consequences, and the divisions between Sunni and Shia were horribly reignited in the aftermath of the US-led invasion of Iraq.

After the attacks of 9/11, Beverley Milton-Edwards warned that a spectre had ascended to trouble the world – the spectre of Islamic

---

11   *The Irish Times*, 2 October 2020.

12   *The Tablet*, 7 July 2018.

13   *The Guardian*, 8 July 2016.

fundamentalism. 'Fundamentalism is a major threat not just in terms of global security but as a manifestation of extreme attachment to faith and religious revivalism at a fanatical level.'[14] As for the question of whether Islam is a religion of peace or a religion to be feared, in the post-9/11 world she said the whole of Islam, despite its rich diversity, was classified in the Western popular imagination as fundamentalist.

> Even when fundamentalist activists speak of, or address, the commonalities between Islam and the West, they are drowned by a hail of bullets or the explosion of the suicide bomb. It appears difficult to reconcile Islam's claim to peace when its leaders are accused of acquiring the technology of destruction. Jihad, not *Salam* (peace) is the word most commonly associated with Islam.
>
> The spectre has undermined and encompasses the whole of Islam and today Islam is classified principally as fundamentalist.[15]

---

14   Beverley Milton-Edwards, *Islamic Fundamentalism Since 1945* (London and New York: Routledge, 2014), p. 10.

15   Ibid., p. 11.

Chapter 18

ISLAM AND ISLAMISM

One day we'll have Islamic law
all over the world.

Taliban commander on CNN, 14 August 2021

Henry Kissinger, who served as US secretary of state in the Nixon and Ford administrations, has provided us with a working definition of Islamism: '[The] modern ideology seeking to enforce Muslim scripture as the central arbiter of personal, political, and international life.'[1]

This appears in a chapter entitled 'Islamism and the Middle East: A World in Disorder' in his book *World Order*. Acknowledging that the Middle East has been the chrysalis of three of the world's great religions, Kissinger then sets out to locate it within the international order along with the challenges this poses.

> The world has been accustomed to calls from the Middle East urging the overthrow of regional and world order in the service of a universal vision. A profusion of prophetic absolutisms has been the hallmark of a region suspended between a dream of its former glory and its contemporary inability to unify around common

---

1   Henry Kissinger, *World Order* (London: Allen Lane, 2014), p. 104.

principles of domestic or international legitimacy. Nowhere is the challenge of international order more complex – in terms of both organising regional order and ensuring the incompatibility of that order with peace and stability in the rest of the world.[2]

Arguably, the great threat today to that order and stability comes from Islamism and all those who embrace it. Islamism keeps alive the dream of a worldwide Muslim international order forged according to the principles of an Islamic State divinely ordained – a universal caliphate.

The three reformers – all intellectuals – whose thinking really gave rise to Islamism were Hasan al-Banna (1906–49), the founder of the Society of Muslims (known colloquially as the Muslim Brotherhood), who was assassinated in 1949; Abul A'la Mawdudi (1903–79), a Pakistani fundamentalist ideologue, and Sayyid Qutb (1906–66), a Muslim Brother executed by Nasser's regime. According to Karen Armstrong, Qutb was the real founder of Islamic fundamentalism in the Sunni world, and was greatly influenced by Mawdudi.[3] A lengthy profile of Qutb by Paul Berman was published in 2003 under the heading 'The Philosopher of Islamic Terror'.[4]

In 1947, al-Banna drafted an Islamic alternative to the secular national state of Egypt. He had founded the Muslim Brotherhood in 1928 to counter what he regarded as the degrading effects of modernity, foreign influence and secular ways of life.

According to Henry Kissinger, al-Banna never clarified how a restored Islamic world order related to the modern international system, built around states.

> Assassinated in 1949, al-Banna was not vouchsafed time to explain in detail how to reconcile the revolutionary ambition of his project of world transformation with the principles of tolerance and cross-civilisational amity that he espoused.

These ambiguities lingered in al-Banna's text, but the record of many Islamic thinkers and movements since then has resolved

---

2   Ibid., p. 96.
3   Karen Armstrong, *Islam: A Short History* (London: Phoenix, 2002), p. 144.
4   *New York Times Magazine*, 23 March 2003.

them in favour of a fundamental rejection of pluralism and secular international order. The religious scholar and Muslim Brotherhood ideologist Sayyid Qutb articulated perhaps the most learned and influential version of this view. In 1964, while imprisoned on charges of participating in a plot to assassinate Egyptian President Nasser, Qutb wrote *Milestones*, a declaration of war against the existing world order that became a foundational text of modern Islamism.

In Qutb's view, Islam was a universal system offering the only true freedom: freedom from government by other men, man-made doctrines, or 'low associations based on race and colour, language and country, regional and national interests' (that is, all other modern forms of governance and loyalty and some of the building blocks of Westphalian order). Islam's modern mission, in Qutb's view, was to overthrow them all and replace them with what he took to be a literal, eventually global implementation of the Qur'an.[5]

Qutb's *Milestones* provided a blueprint and served as a rallying cry for radical Muslims all over the Middle East and beyond. For them it represented, as Kissinger emphasised, 'truths overriding the rules and norms of the Westphalian – or indeed any other – international order'.[6] Karen Armstrong tells us that Qutb went further than Mawdudi in his extremism.

Qutb told Muslims to model themselves on Muhammad: to separate themselves from mainstream society ... and then engage in a violent jihad ... Qutb insisted that the Qur'anic injunction to toleration could only occur *after* the political victory of Islam and the establishment of a true Muslim state. The new intransigence sprang from the profound fear that is at the core of fundamentalist religion. Qutb did not survive. At Nasser's personal insistence, he was executed in 1966.

Every Sunni fundamentalist movement has been influenced by Qutb. The Taliban, who came to power in Afghanistan in 1994,

5   Kissinger, *World Order*, pp. 120–1.
6   Ibid., p. 121.

are also affected by his ideology. They are determined to return to what they see as the original vision of Islam. The ulama are the leaders of the government, women are veiled and not permitted to take part in professional life. Only religious broadcasting is permitted and the Islamic punishments of stoning and mutilation have been reintroduced.[7]

Armstrong wrote this in 2002. It has a fresh relevance now, given that the Taliban are back in power in Afghanistan. 'Most traditional Muslims consider Islamism an errant politicisation of their religion,' according to Maajid Nawaz. He had earlier agreed with a distinction between an Islamist and a jihadist: 'an Islamist attempts to impose his version of Islam on the rest of society, and a jihadist is an Islamist who attempts to do so by force.'[8]

This doesn't sit well with Hirsi Ali: 'I see no difference between Islam and Islamism. Islam is defined as submission to the will of Allah, as it is described in the Qur'an. Islamism is just Islam in its purest form. Sayyid Qutb didn't invent anything, he just quoted the sayings of Muhammad.'[9]

On the broader question of the links between religion and violence, Richard Holloway, the former bishop of Edinburgh and primus of the Scottish Episcopal Church, believes religion does actually *cause* violence, and he insists that this is true not just of Islam but of the three Abrahamic religions – Judaism, Christianity and Islam.

Is religion the main cause of violence in human history, as many have suggested? Religion is certainly no stranger to violence. It has used it in the past and it uses it today. But is it the *cause* of violence? Many thoughtful people think it is ... So yes, religion has caused and continues to cause some of the worst violence in history. And yes, it has used God to justify it. So if we mean by God the loving creator of the universe, then either he doesn't exist or religion has got it wrong.[10]

---

7   Armstrong, *Islam*, pp. 144–5.

8   Sam Harris and Maajid Nawaz, *Islam and the Future of Tolerance: A Dialogue* (Cambridge and London: Harvard University Press, 2015), p. 19. This is a short book that consists of a dialogue between Nawaz and Sam Harris.

9   *The Independent*, 27 November 2007.

10   Richard Holloway, *A Little History of Religion* (New Haven and London: Yale University Press, 2016), p. 231.

Chapter 19

A MUSLIM REFORMATION?

Few great problems of the
world can be solved without an
understanding of how Islam works.

John Laffin

In a 2007 profile of Ayaan Hirsi Ali – a fierce critic of Islam – Andrew Anthony said the Somali-born human rights campaigner 'looks like a fashion model and talks like a public intellectual'. Accompanying the words was a photograph of Hirsi Ali meeting US Secretary of State Condoleezza Rice at *Time* magazine's 100 Most Influential People party in May 2006. Both women had made the 'Leaders & Revolutionaries' list in 2005.

'Tall and slender with rod-straight posture and a schoolgirl smile, she is a thinker of stunning clarity, able to express ideas in her third language with a precision that very few could achieve in their first,' said Anthony.

'This combination of elegance and eloquence would be impressive in any circumstances. Under threat of death, it is nothing short of incredible.'[1]

In 2004, Hirsi Ali had collaborated with the Dutch filmmaker Theo van Gogh (a descendant of the artist Vincent van Gogh) to make a short incendiary film called *Submission*, in which lines from the Qur'an (which

---

1   *The Observer*, 4 February 2007.

Muslims believe is the word of God) detailing a man's right to beat his wife, were projected onto the body of a naked actress. Several weeks after the film aired on Dutch television, van Gogh was shot and stabbed in the centre of Amsterdam in broad daylight. His killer used a knife to pin to his body a letter that called for the death of Hirsi Ali also.

In the midst of the controversy that followed, Hirsi Ali moved to the USA where she became a resident fellow at a Washington think tank, and became a US citizen in 2013.

Born in Mogadishu in November 1969, Hirsi Ali was raised by fundamentalist Muslims. Having been subjected to female genital mutilation (FGM) as a five-year-old child, she was taught from infancy to revere the Prophet Muhammad and the Qur'an. Later she attended a prayer group where the texts of Sayyid Qutb, one of the intellectual inspirations for al-Qaeda, were studied.

In 1991 she moved to Holland and sought asylum when threatened with an arranged marriage to a distant cousin she had never met. The process of 'liberating' herself from Islam gathered pace there; she stopped wearing the hijab, went to bars, gradually dropped the trappings of her culture and religion, and drew inspiration from Mary Wollstonecraft's 1792 classic *A Vindication of the Rights of Women*, John Stuart Mill's *On Liberty* (1859) as well as his essay *On the Subjection of Women* (1869), and the writings of Enlightenment thinkers such as Voltaire (1694–1778). Her first book, *The Caged Virgin*, was published there in 2004 and an English edition appeared in 2006. The book is a rejection of the fanatical form of Islam in which she had been reared, and which promoted culturally and religiously rationalised violence against women. Its publication would make her an internationally prominent critic of Islam.

It is noteworthy, given the traditional subjugation of women in Muslim culture, that Hirsi Ali is one of three women who have emerged as powerful voices urging the need for reform of Islam. The other two are Mona Eltahawy and Irshad Manji. These women take the view that internal reform within Islam is both possible and necessary. According to Hirsi Ali:

> It's wrong to treat Muslims as if they will never find their John Stuart Mill. Christianity and Judaism show that people can be very

dogmatic and then open up ... Can you be a Muslim and respect the separation of Church and State? I hope a large enough number of Muslims will agree you can, and they will find a way to keep the spiritual elements that comfort them and live in a secular society.[2]

All three women have difficulty with the view expressed by Karen Armstrong that 'Islam is not addicted to war, and jihad is not one of its "pillars" or "essential practices".[3] This benign view of Islam, or a view that distinguishes between moderate Islam and Islamism (this latter being a radical ideology in which religion provides the justification for violence) is common.

What if Islam itself is the problem? What if there is a predisposition towards intolerance and violence at the very core of this religion? This is very much the central thesis of *Heretic: Why Islam Needs a Reformation Now*, a 2015 book by Hirsi Ali. In it she boldly challenges centuries of theological and political orthodoxy. At the very outset, she writes this sentence: 'Let me make my point in the simplest possible terms: Islam is not a religion of peace.'[4]

She is well-placed to make this assessment. Although she is now a fellow at Harvard University's John F. Kennedy School of Government, Hirsi Ali has had a chequered personal history. After the 9/11 attacks in New York and Washington DC, she renounced her religion, declaring she was no longer a Muslim. 'I could not overlook the central role the terrorists had attached to Prophet Muhammad as their source of inspiration.' She went on to become an increasingly outspoken critic of the faith she had been born into. She also got a lot of media attention – a black woman who was a fierce critic of Islam. That put her life in danger. She had good reason to be fearful.

In the Islamic world, too many basic rights are being circumscribed, and not only women's rights. Homosexuality is not tolerated. Other religions are not tolerated. Above all, free speech on the subject of Islam is not tolerated. As I only know too well, freethinkers who wish to question works such as the Qur'an or the hadith risk death.[5]

---

2   *The Independent*, 27 November 2007.

3   *Time*, 1 October 2001.

4   Ayaan Hirsi Ali, *Heretic: Why Islam Needs a Reformation Now* (New York: Harper, 2015), p. 3.

5   Ibid., p. 212.

In *The Caged Virgin*, she had already concluded that Islam – a religion that has resisted change for fourteen hundred years – badly needed 'a true Muslim Reformation', drawing a parallel with the sixteenth-century Reformation sparked by Martin Luther that was to transform Christianity. In a chapter entitled 'Let Us Have a Voltaire', she said that Islam required a period of enlightenment and modernisation. 'Where is the biting criticism of Islam from within?' she wondered. 'Does Islam need a Voltaire to call Muslims to break free of superstition, to use their minds and not their emotions, to take note, as he did in the 1800s, that "Nothing can be more contrary to religion and the clergy than reason and common sense"?'[6]

The reality, as John Laffin emphasised in a much earlier book, *The Dagger of Islam*, is that 'criticism from within Islam is rare – and dangerous'.[7] Laffin's book, written long before 9/11 and the rise of al-Qaeda, the Taliban, Islamic State, Boko Haram and al-Shabaab, was really a warning to the West. Hirsi Ali's book echoed that warning, while calling for a radical overhaul of Islam. She identified five key areas where there must be reform:

1. Muhammad's semi-divine and infallible status along with the literalist readings of the Qur'an.
2. The investment in life after death instead of life before death.
3. Sharia law, the body of legislation derived from the Qur'an.
4. The practice of empowering individuals to enforce Islamic law by commanding right and forbidding wrong.
5. The imperative to wage jihad, or holy war.

'All these tenets must be either reformed or discarded.' There is, she argues, a need for a serious discussion of these issues among Muslims themselves. 'That would represent a first step, however hesitant, towards the Reformation that Islam so desperately needs.' For years, ever since 9/11, she has been making a simple argument in response to such acts of terror. 'My argument is that it is foolish to insist, as our leaders habitually do, that

---

6   Ayaan Hirsi Ali, *The Caged Virgin: An Emancipation Proclamation for Women and Islam* (London: Pocket Books, 2007), p. 35.

7   John Laffin, *The Dagger of Islam* (London: Sphere Books, 1979), p. 6.

the violent acts of radical Islamists can be divorced from the religious ideals that inspire them.'[8]

Earlier, in *The Caged Virgin*, she had sought to locate the roots of radical Islam.

> Islamic fundamentalism and political Islam have not suddenly appeared out of nowhere. They needed a breeding ground, where they could take root and grow, before they could be transformed into the dangerous forms that have confronted us since September 11. This breeding ground is created by the way Islam is taught, day in and day out, to Muslims in the Islamic world.[9]

However, the woman named by *Time* magazine as one of the 100 most influential people in the world is under no illusions about the obstacles in the path of an Islamic reformation. 'Innovation of faith is one of the gravest sins in Islam, on a par with murder and apostasy.' However, she stresses that it is important for people in the West to understand what makes Islam fundamentally different from other twenty-first-century monotheistic religions. 'And the starting-point must be the recognition that unreformed Islam is not a religion of peace.'[10]

The task of 'navigating' and balancing the sometimes-conflicting values of freedom of expression and respect for others is especially tortuous when it comes to attitudes within Islam to women's bodies. This is highlighted by debates and conflicts over the hijab (and even more so when it comes to the more extreme forms of dress used by Muslim women, such as the niqab, a veil, usually black, that covers all of the face apart from the eyes, and the burka, the full-length, head-to-toe body covering with just slits for the eyes in the face veil).

In her 2015 book, *Headscarves and Hymens*, Mona Eltahawy, an award-winning journalist and commentator on Arab and Muslim issues, emphasised that the 'act of wearing the hijab is far from simple – it is burdened with meanings'. She went on to explain that 'hijab' is an Arabic

---

8   Hirsi Ali, *Heretic*, p. 2.

9   Hirsi Ali, *The Caged Virgin*, p. 36.

10 Hirsi Ali, *Heretic*, p. 3.

word meaning 'barrier' or 'partition', but 'it has come to represent complex principles of modesty and dress'.

Eltahawy, who was born in Egypt and wore a hijab until she was twenty-five, equates the tradition of imposed veiling to misogyny and points to the power of 'morality police' in places like Sudan and Saudi Arabia to punish women for going unveiled or even wearing trousers. 'I know that nothing frightens Islamists and the equally misogynistic secular men of our society more than the demand for women's rights and sexual freedom.'[11]

She admitted that choosing to wear the hijab was much easier than choosing to take it off, but then poses this key question for those insisting that the headscarf must be worn:

> Why were women alone responsible for sheltering men from the sexual desires women supposedly elicited in men? Why could men not control themselves? Why, if men were the ones being tempted, were they not the ones being policed?[12]

Her book is subtitled 'Why the Middle East Needs a Sexual Revolution', and is a passionate manifesto for change, a courageous call for gender equality. 'The Islamic hatred of women burns brightly across the region – now more than ever'. By 'Islamists' she said she meant an 'advocate or supporter of a political movement that favours reordering government and society in accordance with laws prescribed by Islam'.[13]

She pointed the finger at Saudi Arabia and the austere forms of Islam practised there that made women's lives little short of prison sentences. 'The obsession with controlling women and our bodies often stems from the suspicion that, without restraints, women are just a few degrees short of sexual insatiability'.[14]

Elsewhere, she referred to the popularity of the 'god of virginity' in the Arab world.

---

11   Mona Eltahawy, *Headscarves and Hymens: Why the Middle East Needs a Sexual Revolution* (London: Weidenfeld and Nicolson, 2015), p. 31.

12   Ibid., p. 55.

13   Ibid., p. 11.

14   Ibid.

Everything possible is done to keep the hymen – that most fragile foundation upon which the god of virginity sits – intact. At the altar of the god of virginity, we sacrifice not only our girls' bodily integrity and right to pleasure but also their right to justice in the face of sexual violation. Sometimes we even sacrifice their lives: in the name of 'honour', some families murder their daughters to keep the gods of virginity appeased. When that happens, it leaves one vulnerable to the wonderful temptation of imagining a world where girls and women are more than hymens.[15]

For Eltahawy, who lives in Cairo and New York and who was named by *Newsweek* as one of its 150 Fearless Women of 2012, the controversies over the hijab have convinced her that 'the battle over women's bodies can only be won by a revolution of the mind'.[16] She believes, along with Irshad Manji, that this must be part of a wider reform movement, one that prioritises Islam's need to find a way to accommodate itself to the twenty-first century.

Irshad Manji is a Canadian feminist Muslim whose 2003 book *The Trouble With Islam Today* became an international bestseller (though it was banned throughout the Middle East). 'She is a lesbian feminist Muslim whose ambition is nothing less than to reform Islam. She has been compared by the *New York Times* to Martin Luther; by others to Alexandr Solzhenitsyn, Salman Rushdie, Gloria Steinem and Betty Friedan and, when I met her, socially, by herself to Václav Havel,' said Geraldine Bedell in a long interview in 2008.

What she has to say – that Islam has become calcified and that in its name millions of people around the world are being denied human rights – is offensive to many and troubling even to progressive Muslims and non-Muslims who agree with her but wouldn't say so out loud, for fear of provoking what she calls the beards and the veils.[17]

---

15   Ibid., pp. 114–15.

16   Ibid., p. 31.

17   *The Guardian*, 3 August 2008.

Irshad Manji arrived in Canada with her family at the age of four as a refugee from Idi Amin's Uganda, where she was born in 1968. In time she would go on the study the history of ideas at the University of British Columbia (coming at the top of her class). 'How did she get the nerve to become one of the leading voices demanding reform of one of the world's great religions, at a time when Islam has become so controversial?'[18]

Making the case in her book, Manji says she is seeking to update Islamic interpretations of the Qur'an for the twenty-first century, not the sixteenth.

> Open societies remain open because people take the risk of asking questions – out loud. 'Why is it so easy to draw thousands of Muslims into the streets to denounce France's ban on the hijab, but impossible to draw even a fraction of those demonstrators into the streets to protest Saudi Arabia's *imposition* of the hijab?' And when Muslims insist, 'We're democracies in our own way,' they need to hear this question posed: 'What rights do women and religious minorities exercise in such democracies – not in theory, but in actuality?'[19]

Manji identified three challenges that had to be tackled at the same time. First, the need to revitalise Muslim economies by engaging the talents of women; second, to give 'desert Islam' (the Saudi Arabian version) a run for its money 'by unleashing varied interpretations of Islam'; and third, to 'work with the West, not against it'.[20]

In 2019, the *Daily Telegraph* carried a story by its Asia correspondent Nicola Smith under the heading 'Malay actress "sorry" after she is pictured with no headscarf'. The following are the first four paragraphs of the story:

> A British-Malaysian actress has apologised to fans who were allegedly offended by a photograph circulating on social media where she had removed her headscarf and was seen being friendly towards a man.

---

18   Ibid.

19   Irshad Manji, *The Trouble with Islam Today: A Wake-Up Call for Honesty and Change* (New York: St Martin's Griffin, 2003), p. 192.

20   Ibid., p. 157.

Emma Maembong, 26, who has played the lead role in multiple Malaysian dramas and is so popular that her fans created a club called 'Emanisers', said she was sorry for being careless after the photo went viral.

The actress, who is normally seen in public wearing a Malaysian tudong, which covers the hair, ears and neck, was pictured with her hair flowing and her arm draped over the shoulder of a young male companion, sitting at a dinner table in a restaurant.

The tudong is not compulsory for Malaysian Muslim women, except at the mosque, although most now wear the headscarf following a rise in religious conservatism since the Seventies.[21]

Later in the story, Nicola Smith reported that 'government plans to introduce a dress code for Muslim women in the workplace prompted accusations that officials were acting like fashion police and dehumanising women'.

We are well accustomed by now to stories in the media about controversies involving Muslim women and how they dress in public. In many quarters the kind of body covering many Muslim women wear is seen, rightly or wrongly, as a sign and symbol of their subjection and oppression. This is particularly true of women who wear the burqa – a full-length garment. 'No other item of religious clothing has ignited passions and prejudice among politicians and media commentators as much as the burqa, worn by a minority of Muslim women,' according to Burhan Wazir in a review of a collection of essays by Muslim women on faith, feminism, sexuality and race.[22]

---

21   *The Daily Telegraph*, 29 January 2019.

22   The review of *It's Not About the Burqa* (edited by Mariam Khan) appeared in the *Observer* on 24 March 2019.

Chapter 20

RELIGIOUS LIBERTY

There is no denying that,
whatever the ultimate causes,
killing in the name of religion
represents a moral breakdown.

Martin Woollacott

Whenever people gather to worship in a public place, they are especially vulnerable to attacks by terrorists and extremists, whether the latter are religiously inspired (which they too often are) or not. Sacred spaces, churches, mosques, synagogues and temples should be safe places, but as recent events have tragically shown, they are not.

The dreadful coordinated suicide bombings of churches and hotels in Sri Lanka on Easter Sunday in 2019 – mainly in the capital Colombo – which claimed 269 lives focused attention once again on the central importance of religious freedom. This is a seemingly straightforward concept, but, in reality, is a very nuanced and controversial one.

Christians in particular have been the targets, though not exclusively by any means, as the mass killings in two mosques in Christchurch, New Zealand, in March 2019, which left fifty-one dead, tragically showed. It was Catholic churches that were targeted in Sri Lanka.

Religious persecution has a very long history, as gruesome stories about lions in the Roman Colosseum remind us. However, since the re-emergence of religion as a political force on the world stage following 9/11, intolerance of others' beliefs – if not open hatred of the holders of these beliefs – has been a prominent and deeply troubling feature leading to new forms of religious discrimination, oppression and persecution.

According to the non-partisan Pew Research Center in Washington DC, Christianity remains the world's most persecuted religion, though this is hardly acknowledged in the West. Across the globe Christians are subjected to real and sustained violence because of their faith. As the Rev. Giles Fraser, a Church of England parish priest in London and a regular contributor to BBC Radio 4, noted in the aftermath of the Sri Lanka horrors, during the past century Christianity has been 'all but driven out' of the Middle East, the place of its birth. 'We are now living through one of the most serious phases of Christian persecution in history,' he says, 'and most people refuse to acknowledge it.'

This was backed up shortly afterwards by the publication of a report following a review (launched by the British Foreign Office and led by the Church of England bishop of Truro, the Rt Rev. Philip Mounstephen), which found that 245 million Christians now suffer 'high levels of persecution' in fifty countries as a result of their faith. Bishop Mounstephen warned that Christianity could be 'wiped out' in the Middle East.

We know that Christians are regularly persecuted across much of the Muslim world, from Sudan to Pakistan. So, for that matter, are atheists. Christian and Muslim minorities are brutally repressed in China, and in Myanmar, Muslims are persecuted by Buddhists. Coptic Christians are persecuted in Egypt. The list goes on. What it all demonstrates is that the principle of religious tolerance is (a) a relatively recent one, and (b) is not even acknowledged as an ideal outside of the West. Saudi Arabia, for instance, recognises no religion other than the fundamentalist Wahhabi version of Islam that is the State religion.

It is in churches, mosques, synagogues and temples that people usually congregate to exercise a fundamental human right – the right to freedom of religion. Article 18 of the Universal Declaration of Human Rights (adopted by the UN General Assembly on 10 December 1948) states:

> Everyone has the right to freedom of thought, conscience and religion; this right includes freedom to change his religion or belief, and freedom, either alone or in community with others and

in public or private, to manifest his religion or belief in teaching, practice, worship and observance.

It is not the exclusive right of any one faith, or any one church, though for many centuries it was. Since the time of Emperor Constantine in the fourth century there was one religion – Christianity – in the West. Throughout the Holy Roman Empire, Catholicism (because that was the one version of Christianity), with the papacy at its epicentre, prevailed.

A cosy alliance between the State (personified by the Emperor) and the Church resulted. It suited both sides to work together, to become interdependent. The State would sometimes act as an agent of the Church, by, for instance, enforcing decisions of ecclesiastical courts, such as burning 'heretics' at the stake. The Church, in turn, would lend legitimacy to the State. The notion that there might or ought to somehow be a 'separation' between the two, and that this might even be desirable in certain circumstances, was utterly foreign to both sides.

This doctrine was rudely and dramatically challenged by the first of two epochal events – the Reformation in the early sixteenth century, which gave rise to the birth of Protestantism. Now there was no longer one church with overarching authority over all of Europe. There was now a rival faith, and several rival churches (the English Reformation, engineered by King Henry VIII, spawned that form of Protestantism known as Anglicanism – with the newly created Church of England as its mother church). Henceforth, the popes no longer spoke for all of Christendom.

Hostility between the rival faiths spilled over into the terrible violence of the 'wars of religion' which scarred Europe for decades and cost the lives of millions. Eventually, a solution of sorts was arrived at through the Treaty of Westphalia of 1648, which brought to an end the final phase of the religious strife known as the Thirty Years War.

Martin Luther's rebellion of 1517 had directly challenged the papal monarchy. Pope Boniface VIII (1294–1303) had claimed jurisdiction for the papacy throughout the whole world in the papal bull of 1302, *Unam sanctam* – 'One Holy (Church)'. 'This was a culminating moment in the universal pretensions of the papacy,' says Diarmaid MacCulloch, professor of the history of the church at Oxford University.

In the aftermath of a second epochal event – the French Revolution of 1789 to 1815 – far from seeing an abandonment of these pretensions, they were intensified. The Revolution had led not just to the dethronement of Europe's most powerful Catholic monarch, Louis XVI, but to his execution (January 1793). Little wonder that this appalled and horrified the other Catholic monarchs in Europe, as well as the monarch in Rome – the pope.

By the middle of the nineteenth century, alarmed by the spreading tide of liberalism unleashed by the French Revolution, Rome decided to react. Already in 1832, Pope Gregory XVI had issued an encyclical, *Mirari vos* ('Wonder at you'), in which he denounced the notions of freedom of conscience and of the press, and of the separation of Church and State. But in 1864 there would be a much more trenchant rejection of liberal values and modernising political currents when Pope Pius IX issued an encyclical, *Quanta cura* ('Condemning current errors'), to which was attached a *Syllabus of Errors* condemning, among other things, the principle that non-Catholics should be given freedom of religion in a Catholic State.

Along with religious liberty, Pius IX also condemned liberty of conscience and the separation of Church and State, and rejected the proposition that the pope 'can and ought to reconcile himself with progress, liberalism and modern civilisation'. The papacy would cling to the old model of Church–State relations – stemming from the 'happy marriage of Altar and Throne' (as historians of Christianity would describe it). For centuries, popes had reiterated the principle *Extra ecclesiam nulla salus* ('Outside the Church there is no salvation'). An offspring of this was the doctrine that 'error has no rights'.

Prior to the Reformation, the principle and the doctrine would go virtually uncontested. In the post-Reformation period, and especially since the Peace of Augsburg of 1555, which recognised 'confessional states' in both Protestant and Catholic Europe, the situation became much more complicated. According to the formula agreed at Augsburg, the ruler (monarch) determined the religion of the territory he controlled – *cuius regio, eius religio* ('whose realm, his religion'). The formula provided that in each territory subjects should follow the religion of their rulers.

For Rome and the papacy, however, the claim of 'one true church' remained unshaken. It would be buttressed in 1870 when the controversial

Syllabus of 1864 was followed by the solemn declaration at the First Vatican Council of papal primacy and infallibility. The concept of Church–State relations that followed has been well outlined by Professor John W. O'Malley of Georgetown University:

> The basic premise of the teaching was that only truth has a right to freedom, or, put negatively, as it often was, 'error has no rights'. In essence the teaching boiled down to the following. First, if the majority of the citizens were Catholics, the State had the duty to profess the Catholic faith and do all it reasonably could to promote and defend it. This meant that at the same time it was duty-bound to discourage or even suppress other religions, which might include denying their adherents some civil rights.
>
> Second, in certain situations, 'in order to avoid greater evils', it might be necessary to tolerate other religions and thus allow their free practice. Third, when Catholics are in a minority, the State has the duty from natural law to guarantee them full citizenship and free practice of their religion because the State must foster the pursuit of truth, which the Catholic Church possesses.[1]

It wasn't until the twentieth century that this doctrine of Church–State relations became unstuck. Theologians in France and the United States, in particular, began to make a case for a revision of this doctrine in the light of changed political realities. The decision by John F. Kennedy to run for the American presidency in 1960 proved to be a game changer. At that time, the prospect of a Catholic being in the White House for the very first time caused great unease, especially within the US Protestant churches. Fears of 'Rome rule' began to be voiced. 'No Catholic, critics claimed, could be president because he would have to obey the Church and work for the suppression of all religions except Catholicism,' explained Professor O'Malley.[2]

In view of the flare-up of anti-Catholic sentiment during his campaign, Kennedy travelled to Houston, Texas, on 12 September 1960 where he

---

1   John W. O'Malley, *What Happened at Vatican II* (Cambridge and London: Harvard University Press, 2010), p. 212.

2   Ibid., p. 213.

delivered a landmark speech to a large gathering of Baptist ministers. In the course of the thirty-minute speech, which was widely praised afterwards, he reaffirmed in ringing terms the separation of Church and State, decried any mixing of religion and politics, and vowed, if elected, never to let his religious views influence his decisions as president. If he were ever required as president 'either to violate my conscience or violate the national interest, then I would resign the office'. Kennedy went on to say that he believed in an America where 'religious liberty is so indivisible that an act against one church is treated as an act against all'.

By 1960 preparations were already underway in Rome for the Second Vatican Council, which had been convened by Pope John XXIII. It would produce a document that would reflect the new thinking that had emerged on religious liberty and its implications for Church–State relations.

In view of all that had gone before, the concept of religious liberty is one that has only found formal acknowledgement and acceptance within the Catholic Church since 1965 when, on the day before it ended, the Second Vatican Council's *Declaration on Religious Liberty* was promulgated by Pope Paul VI.

The principal architect of this historic declaration, the man who laid the groundwork for it, was the American Jesuit John Courtney Murray. He was well aware that in 1960 the official Catholic teaching on Church–State relations was an obstacle raised during JFK's presidential campaign. In the 1950s Murray had begun writing about the need for a new approach, more in line with what was required in a modern democratic society where religious pluralism was a reality. The Catholic Church should be seeking to promote religious liberty, not suppress it. This would eventually land him in trouble with the Holy Office during the pontificate of Pius XII (later renamed the Congregation for the Doctrine of the Faith), and under pressure from that office his Jesuit superiors instructed him to cease publishing.

Murray was convinced that America had proved by experience that political unity and stability were possible without uniformity of religious belief and practice, and without the necessity of any governmental restrictions on any religion. His opponents in Rome didn't think this could be reconciled with Church teaching that proclaimed there was only one true religion, and thus did not admit freedom of choice. Professor Charles

Curran of the Catholic University of America had summed up the situation Murray faced: 'The American democratic system proposed separation of Church and State and espoused religious liberty, whereas Roman Catholicism called for union of Church and State and refused to accept religious freedom.'[3] With Rome very suspicious of the American system, Murray faced an uphill struggle. Powerful figures in Rome looked on him and his writings as heretical.

The election of John XXIII in 1958 and the calling of Vatican II meant rehabilitation for Murray and his writings, and the Pope personally appointed him to the panel of experts for two of the Council's great documents – the *Pastoral Constitution on the Church in the Modern World*, and the *Declaration on Religious Liberty*. However, when the latter came to be debated on the floor of the Council, there was still bitter opposition to it. It was seen by some of its opponents as a betrayal of past papal teaching.

Prior to the Council, popes had vehemently opposed freedom of conscience, religious liberty and the separation of Church and State. The most noteworthy example of this, as we have seen, was Pius XI's *Syllabus of Errors*, published in 1864. Yet it was another pope, John XXIII, who in his 1963 encyclical *Pacem in terris* ('Peace on Earth') pointed the way forward when he spoke of the human right to worship God 'according to the dictates of an upright conscience'. In other words, the freedom to follow one's conscience in religious matters must be genuine, not coerced. According to Curran:

> The genius of John Courtney Murray was to confront the former Catholic position and show that a development of Catholic teaching in the light of historical circumstances could fully accept the American position of separation of Church and State and espouse religious liberty. The *Declaration on Religious Liberty* of the Second Vatican Council crowned his work with success.[4]

The Declaration itself acknowledged that 'the right to religious liberty is based on the dignity of the human person ... This right of the individual

---

3   Charles E. Curran, *American Catholic Social Ethics* (Notre Dame and London: University of Notre Dame Press, 1982), p. 179.

4   Ibid., p. 176.

to religious liberty must be granted that recognition in the constitutional ordering of society which will make it a civil right.' It went on to say, 'It is agreed then that modern man wants to be able to profess his religion freely, in private and in public; in fact, religious liberty has already been declared a civil right in the majority of constitutions and been given solemn recognition in international documents.'

However, freedom of religion, as an editorial in the *Guardian* immediately after the Sri Lanka bombings reminded us, is

> a surprisingly complex idea, because it isn't only the apparently unproblematic freedom to believe whatever you want. It couldn't just be that. Religions bind belief to action. They deal in moral questions as well as metaphysical and social ones, and moral beliefs are about what we should do and how we should treat other people. As such, they can't be private. They affect the world outside of our minds. This is not a problem that any society can solve by saying that everyone should live according to their own code of morality, for moral injunctions ought by their nature to be binding on everyone. To take some obviously contested examples from the contemporary culture wars: if either racism, or abortion, are always and everywhere wrong, then they should be always and everywhere forbidden, and those who believe in them should have their freedom to act on these beliefs restricted. That is why in the UK there are laws restricting hate speech, while in parts of the US there are laws restricting abortion instead. Yet these restrictions are not persecution. There is a vital distinction between preventing someone from acting on their beliefs and punishing them for believing in the first place.[5]

The concept of religious liberty is a key element of the doctrine of the separation of Church and State, a doctrine that is usually traced back to Thomas Jefferson, the USA's third president (1801–9), who advocated the building of a 'wall of separation' between the two. It is an American creation.

---

5   *The Guardian*, 22 April 2019.

Professor Stephen Carter of Yale University has described the separation of Church and State as 'one of the great gifts that American political philosophy has presented to the world'.[6] The Catholic Church, however, in and through Vatican II – very belatedly, some would say, given the Catholic Church's previous history, which includes the Crusades and the Inquisition – made a hugely important contribution to the modern understanding of it. Sadly, as recent events have tragically shown, it is a doctrine that in the twenty-first century is still very far from being universally acknowledged and accepted.

---

6   Stephen L. Carter, *The Culture of Disbelief: How American Law and Politics Trivialize Religious Devotion* (New York: Anchor Books, 1994), p. 107.

Chapter 21

GOD'S OWN COUNTRY

Religion remains an important
political factor in the United States.

**Kenneth D. Wald and
Allison Calhoun-Brown**

An edition of *Newsweek* magazine in November 2006 had a striking photograph on its front cover – it showed a cross tightly wrapped in the Stars and Stripes. The title of the cover story was 'America's God Complex'. Inside, the following line appeared: 'America's political system has increasingly fallen under the sway of Christian evangelicals.'[1]

In a world where Church leaders such as the pope and the archbishop of Canterbury are alarmed at the spread of secularisation in Europe, it is astonishing that, even in the twenty-first century, no candidate in the USA can expect to be elected to the White House without playing the 'God card'.

Unlike Europe, the USA remains an intensely religious society. 'One of the most interesting puzzles in the sociology of religion is why Americans are so much more religious as well as more churchly than Europeans,' according to Peter L. Berger.[2]

---

1   *Newsweek*, 13 November 2006.

2   Peter L. Berger, ed., *The Desecularization of the World: Resurgent Religion and World Politics* (Grand Rapids: WB Eerdmans Publishing Company, 1999), p. 10.

Even Sam Harris, one of the militant new atheists whose books sell very well, has had to concede this. 'Despite the explicit separation of Church and State provided for by the US Constitution, the level of religious belief in the United States (and the concomitant significance of religion in American life and political discourse) rivals that of many theocracies.'[3]

This is the main reason why candidates for high office seek to outdo each other in establishing and displaying their religious credentials. Even former president Donald Trump – regarded by his critics as the most profane, religiously illiterate president in the country's history – knew the importance of playing the 'God card'. One of the abiding images of his presidency was a photograph of him standing in front of St John's Episcopal Church (a small nineteenth-century building known as 'the church of the presidents' across from the White House) with a Bible in his hand. According to Frank Bruni in 2013:

> You can make a successful run for political office in this country without an especially thick resumé, any exceptional talent for expressing yourself, a noteworthy education or, for that matter, a basic grasp of science. But you better have religion. You better be ready to profess your faith in and fealty to God – the Judea-Christian one, of course. And you better be convincing.[4]

All candidates for the White House ignore, at their peril, the vast religious constituency spread across the USA. 'Religion has been inseparable from American politics for as long as America has had politics,' according to Stephen Carter, professor of law at Yale University, 'and will likely remain inseparable as long as Americans remain religious.'

The same, of course, could be said of Ireland where the interface between religion and politics has been a central characteristic of the culture in both parts of the island, though the consequences of such an interface have had diverse effects North and South.

---

3   Sam Harris, *The Moral Landscape: How Science can Determine Human Values* (London: Bantam Press, 2010), p. 145.

4   *The New York Times*, 7 December 2017.

One of the big differences, however, between Ireland and USA is that the latter, from its very founding, has nurtured a conviction that it was 'God's own country' and destined to be a beacon of liberty to the rest of the world.

The pilgrims who set sail from England in the seventeenth century onboard the *Mayflower* and other vessels to settle in America were imbued with a religious zeal that has coloured American civic life and politics ever since. The Mayflower Compact of 1620 contains this passage: 'Having undertaken for the glory of God, and the Advancement of the Christian Faith ... a voyage to plant the first colony in the northern part of Virginia ...' In 1630, onboard another pilgrim ship, the *Arabella*, John Winthrop addressed his fellow travellers off the coast of Massachusetts as follows: 'We shall be as a city upon a hill – the eyes of all people are upon us.' Winthrop's phrase comes straight from the account of the Sermon on the Mount in the Gospel of Matthew (5:14): 'Ye are the light of the world. A city that is set on a hill cannot be hid.' The belief that America has been the recipient of God's favour took root. The conviction that the USA is indeed 'God's own country' has been deeply embedded in American culture and politics ever since.

This interplay between religion and politics in America is unique among Western nations. What Professor Carter has called 'the injection of religion into politics' has led to 'the development of a Christian litmus test for those seeking the White House'.

In *The Mighty and the Almighty*, Madeleine Albright addressed the question of why religion cannot be kept out of politics.

> My answer is that we can't and shouldn't. Religion is a large part of what motivates people and shapes their view of justice and right behaviour. It must be taken into account. Nor can we expect our leaders to make decisions in isolation from their religious beliefs. There is a limit to how much the human mind can compartmentalise. In any case, why should world leaders who are religious act and speak as if they are not.[5]

---

5   Madeleine Albright, *The Mighty and the Almighty: Reflections on America, God, and World Affairs* (London: Pan Books, 2007), p. 283.

The republican impulse to separate Church and State is motivated primarily by a desire to prevent or nullify the emergence or growth of political religion or what some scholars refer to as 'faith-based politics'. But the separation doctrine doesn't mean 'that people whose motivations are religious are banned from trying to influence government, nor that government is banned from listening to them'.[6]

Secularists envisage a scenario in which religion and politics may co-exist like parallel lines but where there is no crossover; they do not intermix or interact. That may be fine in theory but the reality throughout the world is very different. Even in avowedly Communist countries like Russia, China, Cuba and Vietnam religion is, however reluctantly, tolerated. It may be driven underground, but it has not been eradicated. It continues to influence the lives and behaviour of people, even though they may only constitute a small minority, as in China. It is true that religion is excluded from the 'public square' (Russia is an exception here), but it has a social presence nevertheless.

In Vladimir Putin's Russia there is now a very clear alliance between the Putin-led administration and the Russian Orthodox Church. In Stalin's Russia, just as in Mao's China, years of brutal oppression and persecution failed to wipe out religion, so today in both countries an accommodation of sorts has been arrived at. This is far more visible and substantive in Russia, but in both places the lessons of the failure of Stalin and Mao to eradicate religion have been learned.

In Moscow, Putin now regards the Russian Orthodox Patriarch, Kirill I, as an ally, and the Church is looked on almost as a department of State. In March 2019, the Kremlin reported that Putin had 'dipped into his own pocket' to pay for a religious icon to adorn a new Russian Orthodox cathedral near Moscow dedicated to the country's military.

It was a protest against this cosy relationship between Church and State that brought Pussy Riot global notoriety. On 21 February 2012, five members of the feminist punk band staged an obscenity-laced performance of their 'Punk Prayer' in the Cathedral of Christ the Saviour in Moscow. Orthodox clergy condemned the protest as 'sacrilegious' and there were

---

6   Stephen L. Carter, *The Culture of Disbelief: How American Law and Politics Trivialize Religious Devotion* (New York: Anchor Books, 1994), p. 106.

calls for the introduction of a blasphemy law. Members of Pussy Riot were arrested and charged with hate crimes and violations of public order. Three were imprisoned. Writing later that year of the protest, Jeffrey Taylor said: 'Patriarch Kirill has moved the Church ever closer to the Kremlin and, ahead of presidential elections last March, openly called on Russians to vote for Putin.'[7]

On the eve of Patriarch Kirill's first visit to the UK in 2016, Michael Binyon of the *Daily Telegraph*, wrote:

> Since the fall of communism, the Kremlin has embraced the Russian Orthodox Church ever more closely. President Putin has made a show of piety, being frequently pictured with Church leaders and speaking openly of the role of the Church in upholding and strengthening Russia's moral values and cultural identity.
>
> In turn, Church leaders play a prominent role on State occasions, have blessed the work of Russia's leaders and are vocal in backing the country's policies overseas.
>
> Patriarch Kirill has been particularly supportive of Mr Putin, calling his era a 'miracle of God' in 2012 and urging Russians to vote for him during the election that year.[8]

What the Russian invasion of Ukraine in February 2022 showed unmistakably was that Kirill's support for Putin extended even to war-making. 'Christian churches have from time immemorial colluded with political ambition and expansionism, be that imperialist, nationalist or economic, providing each with ideological justification, and benefitting in social leverage in return,' explained Very Rev. Maria Jansson, the retired Church of Ireland dean of Waterford in the aftermath of Russian invasion of Ukraine.

> This phenomenon has reared its ugly head again in the person of Patriarch Kirill of Moscow and all Russia, leader of 110 million

---

7   *Atlantic Magazine*, 8 November 2012.

8   *The Daily Telegraph*, 8 October 2016.

Russian Orthodox Christians and who has been an ardent supporter of Vladimir Putin since he came to power ... Kirill refuses to condemn the invasion of Ukraine, despite repeated calls for him to do so from Pope Francis, other Orthodox Church leaders and more recently from the World Council of Churches.[9]

The Patriarch's refusal is just a further but deeply unsettling example of 'political religion' taken to extremes. What it reinforces is the acknowledgement by Linda Hogan, professor of ecumenics at Trinity College Dublin, that religion is 'here to stay, and its impact on political life is likely to persist in multiple forms'.[10]

---

9   *The Irish Times*, 11 April 2022.

10   *The Irish Times*, 4 July 2015.

Chapter 22

RELIGIOUS HEALING

More often seen as a source of conflict,
religion is generally overlooked as a potential
resource in promoting global diplomacy.

Mary McAleese

In his novel *The Shoes of the Fisherman* – first published in 1963[1] – Morris West has a scene where the fictional central character, Pope Kirill I (from Ukraine) establishes a back channel between the leaders of the Soviet Union and the USA in order to avert a nuclear war.

In 1963 the Cold War had led to very dangerous tensions between the East and the West. The Cuban Missile Crisis of October 1962 had brought the confrontation between the USA and the USSR to the brink of nuclear catastrophe. In the Vatican, Pope John XXIII issued his famous encyclical *Pacem in terris* ('Peace on Earth') in April 1963.

Morris West was writing against a background of great mistrust, suspicion, uncertainty and fear on the international front. A year after the Cuban Revolution of 1959 and the establishment of a revolutionary state by Fidel Castro, President Dwight Eisenhower broke off diplomatic ties with Havana after Castro had nationalised American-owned banks in Cuba.

---

1   Morris West, *The Shoes of the Fisherman* (London: Pan Books, 1963).

Relations between the two countries continued to deteriorate over the following decades as the USA under various presidents tightened sanctions and its embargo on trade. However, in February 2008, when Fidel Castro, whose health was declining, handed over the presidency to his brother, Raúl, the Obama administration hinted that, given meaningful democratic change in Cuba, the US was prepared to take steps to normalise relations. Then, on 17 December 2014, Barack Obama and Raúl Castro announced they would restore full diplomatic ties. This followed eighteen months of secret talks between US and Cuban officials that were brokered, in part, by Pope Francis. In July 2015 the United States and Cuban embassies, which had been closed since 1961, reopened.

A normally reticent Holy See released a short statement in the summer of 2014 acknowledging the Pope's role:

> In recent months, Pope Francis wrote letters to the President of the Republic of Cuba, His Excellency Mr Raúl Castro, and the President of the US, the Honourable Barack H. Obama, and invited them to resolve humanitarian questions of common interest, including the situation of certain prisoners, in order to initiate a new phase in relations between the two parties. The Holy See received delegations of the two countries in the Vatican last October and provided its good offices to facilitate a constructive dialogue on delicate matters, resulting in solutions acceptable to both parties.[2]

Later, in a press conference, Cardinal Pietro Parolin, the Vatican secretary of state, stated that Pope Francis had played a key role in facilitating and promoting dialogue between the United States and Cuba.

Was this a case of fact following fiction? Morris West's imaginary intervention by a pope certainly demonstrated how far-seeing he was, but the part played by Pope Francis showed how, to use Mary McAleese's words, religion could be a resource in promoting global diplomacy. This was precisely the case made and developed in a 2021 book entitled *On the Significance of Religion for Global Diplomacy.*

---

2   cruxnow.com, 17 December 2014.

The four authors – Philip McDonagh, John Neary (both of whom are former Irish ambassadors), Kishan Manocha and Lucia Vázquez Mendoza – make a series of recommendations linking religion, peace and diplomacy, as well as a comprehensive blueprint for achieving this:

> Freedom of religion or belief is a core value in our societies. 'Religious literacy' is already acknowledged as a necessary diplomatic skill. It is time to enable a deeper engagement by public authorities with religious perspectives as a resource in global peace building and diplomacy. 'Social capital' and other features of a strong political culture are also a primary focus of the world's religions.[3]

In a column in the *Irish Times*, another retired diplomat, Carmel Heaney, outlined why religion has a role to play in global affairs, echoing some of the themes dealt with by the four authors.

> In 1990, Samuel Huntington had predicted, in his book *The Clash of Civilisations and the Remaking of World Order*, that future wars would be fought not about territory but between conflicting cultures, in which religion is deeply embedded. Responding, former Iranian president Mohammad Khatami proposed a dialogue among civilisations, expressing the determination to facilitate international discussion.
>
> The challenge involved in such aspirations was starkly demonstrated by the attack on the World Trade Center in September 2001. The war on terror followed, but so, slowly, did a new realisation that religion, in its capacity for the therapeutic as well as the toxic, needs to be addressed as a factor in international affairs.[4]

---

3   Philip McDonagh, Kishan Manocha, John Neary and Lucia Vázquez Mendoza, *On the Significance of Religion for Global Diplomacy* (London and New York: Routledge, 2021), p. xix.

4   *The Irish Times*, 8 June 2021.

Chapter 23

AFTERTHOUGHTS: RELIGION AND THE FUTURE

In the years since 9/11, it has become
clear that religion is part and parcel of the
unfolding of twenty-first-century history.

Malory Nye

It is surely ironic that as indifference to and disengagement from religion grows in Ireland, the need to understand religion, its politico-cultural significance, its enduring appeal for millions around the globe, and its role in society is being increasingly recognised by academics, diplomats, government advisers and policymakers in the major capitals of the world.

Some of the reasons for this reawakened interest may be negative – a reaction to the rise of radical Islam and, in particular, to the toxic embodiment of this in al-Qaeda, Isis, the Taliban, and al-Shabaab, and other groups with their cult of death.

In the largely secularised Europe, where religion has been either pushed out altogether from the public square or largely marginalised where the formation of public policy is concerned, there is a new urgency – driven largely by incomprehension but also by uncertainty and fear – to get to grips with the phenomenon of a religion-driven ideology.

Not that long ago, few policymakers in the West cared very much what a caliphate meant – after all, hadn't that died with the demise of the Ottoman

Empire, being formally abolished by Mustafa Kemal ('Atatürk') in his new Republic of Turkey in 1923?

A caliphate is a form of Islamic government led by a caliph, a person considered a religious and political successor to the Prophet Muhammad, and claiming to be the leader of the entire Muslim community. The caliph needs a territory or state over which he can exercise jurisdiction. Given the bloody experiences of an Islamic State caliphate in Syria, and the return to power of the Taliban in Afghanistan, policymakers in the West care very much about all forms of Islamic government.

What is becoming increasingly evident is that we live in a world where religion is very important: nearly every news bulletin is a reminder of this. In his preface to a collection of essays on global religions, Christopher Partridge, professor of contemporary religion at University College Chester, emphasised the importance of religion today.

> In the small, complicated world of the twenty-first century, there is a widespread and growing awareness of the significance of religions and beliefs. Not only have religions contributed to the foundations of civilisations throughout history, but also they have directly influenced contemporary international relations and significant world events.[1]

This is true in 2023 to a degree that would have shocked the leading intellectuals of the Enlightenment (sometimes called 'The Age of Reason'), who believed they had sounded religion's death knell. When Marx and Engels came to publish *The Communist Manifesto* in 1848, they were convinced that God had indeed been banished, and religion would soon be redundant. In this respect at least, they couldn't have been more wrong.

The findings of the Pew Research Center, published in 2015 in a survey entitled 'The Future of World Religions: Population Growth Projections 2010–2050', would have dispelled any doubts about the growth of religion in the twenty-first century. Pew is a widely respected non-partisan think tank based in Washington DC, and it found in its survey that 'over the next four decades

---

1   Christopher Partridge, ed., *The World's Religions* (Oxford: Lion, 2005), p. 9.

Christians will remain the largest group in the world, but Islam will grow faster than any other major religion. If current trends continue, by 2050 the number of Muslims will nearly equal the number of Christians around the world.'

Pew reported that, as of 2010, Christianity was by far the world's largest religion, with an estimated 2.2 billion adherents, nearly a third (31%) of all 6.9 billion on earth. Islam was second, with 1.6 billion adherents, or 23% of the global population.

> If current trends continue, however, Islam will nearly catch up by the middle of the twenty-first century. Between 2010 and 2050, the world's total population is expected to rise to 9.3 billion, a 35% increase. Over that same period, Muslims – a comparatively youthful population with high fertility rates – are projected to increase by 73%. The number of Christians is also expected to rise, but more slowly, at about the same rate (35%) as the global population overall.
>
> As a result, by 2050 there will be near parity between Muslims (2.8 billion, or 30% of the population) and Christians (2.9 billion, or 31%), possibly for the first time in history.
>
> With the exceptions of Buddhists, all the world's major religious groups are poised for at least some growth in absolute numbers in the coming decades. The global Buddhist population is expected to be fairly stable because of low fertility rates and ageing populations in countries such as China, Thailand and Japan.
>
> Worldwide, the Hindu population is projected to rise by 34%, from a little over a billion to nearly 1.4 billion, roughly keeping pace with overall population growth. Jews, the smallest group for which separate projections were made, are expected to grow by 16% from a little less than 14 million in 2010 to 16.1 million worldwide in 2050 …
>
> Atheists, agnostics and other people who do not affiliate with any religion – though increasing in countries such as the United States and France – will make up a declining share of the world's total population.[2]

---

2 'The Future of World Religions: Population Growth Projections, 2010–2050', Pew Research Center, https://www.pewresearch.org/religion/2015/04/02/religious-projections-2010-2050/ (accessed April 2022).

The significance of this is that the secularised, religionless world so memorably envisioned by John Lennon in his song 'Imagine' was, as he himself suspected, just a dream. Far from disappearing, religion is going to play an increasingly significant role in international relations, and in the decades ahead, religion – especially 'political religion' – will exercise a potent influence on world affairs.

That said, the great challenge for the future will be to discover how, in the words of Madeleine Albright, 'we can do a better job of using religion to promote global civility'.[3] Earlier she had reminded readers of this key point: 'Religion at its best can reinforce the core values necessary for people from different cultures to live in some degree of harmony; we should make the most of that possibility.'

The former vice-chairman of the National Intelligence Council at the CIA, Graham E. Fuller, has highlighted why we cannot be indifferent to the role of religion in life and the importance of the relationship of religion to politics.

> When religion is linked with politics, two of the most vital elements of human concern come together. This conjuncture can be for better or for worse: both religion and politics have consistently exploited each other across the web of history. Indeed, how could politics ever remain indifferent to such a powerful motive force as religion? And how could religion, with its vision of the place of human existence in the grand scheme of things, remain uninterested in the form, expression, and direction of human society and politics?[4]

---

3   Madeleine Albright, *The Mighty and the Almighty: Reflections on America, God, and World Affairs* (London: Pan Books, 2007), p. 292.

4   Graham E. Fuller, *The Future of Political Islam* (New York: Palgrave Macmillan, 2003), p. xiii.

Select Bibliography

Albright, Madeleine, *The Mighty and the Almighty: Reflections on America, God, and World Affairs* (London: Pan Books, 2007).

Allen, Charles, *God's Terrorists: The Wahhabi Cult and the Hidden Roots of Modern Jihad* (London: Little, Brown, 2006).

Armstrong, Karen, *Islam: A Short History* (London: Phoenix, 2002).

Armstrong, Karen, *Muhammad: A Biography of the Prophet* (London: A W&N Paperback, 2001).

Armstrong, Karen, *The Case for God: What Religion Really Means* (New York and London: Vintage Books, 2010).

Armstrong, Karen, *Fields of Blood: Religion and the History of Violence* (London: The Bodley Head, 2014).

Bernstein, Carl and Marco Politi, *His Holiness: John Paul II and the Hidden History of Our Time* (London and New York: Doubleday, 1996).

Berger, Peter L., ed., *The Desecularization of the World: Resurgent Religion and World Politics* (Grand Rapids: WB Eerdmans Publishing Company, 1999).

Bowker, John, *Religion Hurts: Why Religions do Harm as well as Good* (London: SPCK, 2018).

Burke, Jason, *Al-Qaeda: The True Story of Radical Islam* (London: Penguin Books, 2007).

Burleigh, Michael, *The Third Reich: A New History* (London: Pan Books, 2001).

Carter, Stephen L., *The Culture of Disbelief: How American Law and Politics Trivialize Religious Devotion* (New York: Anchor Books, 1994).

Carter, Stephen L., *God's Name in Vain: The Wrongs and Rights of Religion in Politics* (New York: Basic Books, 2000).

Chomsky, Noam, *Who Rules the World?* (London: Penguin Books, 2017).

Cockburn, Patrick, *The Rise of Islamic State: ISIS and the New Sunni Revolution* (London: Verso, 2015).

Cooney, John, *John Charles McQuaid: Ruler of Catholic Ireland* (Dublin: The O'Brien Press, 1999).

Cooney, John, *The American Pope: The Life and Times of Francis Cardinal Spellman* (New York: Times Books, 1984).

Cornwell, John, *The Pope in Winter: The Dark Face of John Paul II's Papacy* (London: Penguin Books, 2005).

Cruise O'Brien, Conor, *Memoir: My Life and Themes* (Dublin: Poolbeg, 1999).

Curran, Charles E., *American Catholic Social Ethics* (Notre Dame and London: University of Notre Dame, 1982).

De Botton, Alain, *Religion for Atheists: A Non-Believer's Guide to the Uses of Religion* (London: Hamish Hamilton, 2012).

Dillon, Martin, *God and the Gun: The Church and Irish Terrorism* (New York: Routledge, 1999).

Duffy Toft, Monica, Daniel Philpott and Timothy Samuel Shah, *God's Century: Resurgent Religion and Global Politics* (New York and London: WW Norton and Company, 2011).

Elliott, Marianne, *When God Took Sides: Religion and Identity in Ireland* (Oxford: Oxford University Press, 2009).

Eltahawy, Mona, *Headscarves and Hymens: Why the Middle East Needs a Sexual Revolution* (London: Weidenfeld and Nicolson, 2015).

Ferriter, Diarmaid, *The Transformation of Ireland 1900–2000* (London: Profile Books, 2005).

Filby, Eliza, *God and Mrs Thatcher: The Battle for Britain's Soul* (London: Biteback Publishing, 2015).

Flannery, Austin, ed., *Vatican Council II: The Basic Sixteen Documents* (Dublin: Dominican Publications, 1996).

Foster, RF, *Modern Ireland 1600–1972* (London: Penguin Books, 1989).

Fuller, Graham E., *The Future of Political Islam* (New York: Palgrave Macmillan, 2003).

Fuller, Louise, *Irish Catholicism Since 1950: The Undoing of a Culture* (Dublin: Gill and Macmillan, 2004).

Green, Vivian HH, *Luther and the Reformation* (London: New English Library, 1974).

Grzymala-Busse, Anna, *Nations Under God: How Churches Use Moral Authority to Influence Policy* (Princeton and Oxford: Princeton University Press, 2015).

Harris, Sam, *The Moral Landscape: How Science can Determine Human Values* (London: Bantam Press, 2010).

Harris, Sam and Maajid Nawaz, *Islam and the Future of Tolerance: A Dialogue* (Cambridge and London: Harvard University Press, 2015).

Hirsi Ali, Ayaan, *The Caged Virgin: An Emancipation Proclamation for Women and Islam* (London: Pocket Books, 2007).

Hirsi Ali, Ayaan, *Heretic: Why Islam Needs a Reformation Now* (New York: Harper, 2015).

Holloway, Richard, *A Little History of Religion* (New Haven and London: Yale University Press, 2016).

Inglis, Tom, *Moral Monopoly: The Rise and Fall of the Catholic Church in Modern Ireland* (Dublin: University College Dublin Press, 1998) (2nd edn).

Juergensmeyer, Mark, *Terror in the Mind of God: The Global Rise of Religious Violence* (California: University of California Press, 2001).

Keogh, Dermot, *Ireland and the Vatican: The Politics and Diplomacy of Church–State Relations, 1922–1960* (Cork: Cork University Press, 1995).

Kepel, Gilles, *The War for Muslim Minds: Islam and the West* (Cambridge and London: Harvard University Press, 2004).

Khan, Mariam, ed., *It's Not About the Burqa* (London: Picador, 2019).

Kissinger, Henry, *World Order* (London: Allen Lane, 2014).

Laffin, John, *The Dagger of Islam* (London: Sphere Books, 1979).

Lee, JJ, *Ireland 1912–1985: Politics and Society* (Cambridge: Cambridge University Press, 1989).

Lewis, James R., ed., *The Cambridge Companion to Religion and Terrorism* (Cambridge: Cambridge University Press, 2017).

MacCulloch, Diarmaid, *The Reformation: A History* (London: Penguin Books, 2005).

MacCulloch, Diarmaid, *A History of Christianity* (London: Penguin Books, 2009).

Manji, Irshad, *The Trouble with Islam Today: A Wake-Up Call for Honesty and Change* (New York: St Martin's Griffin, 2003).

Miller, William D., *Dorothy Day: A Biography* (San Francisco: Harper and Row, 1982).

Milton-Edwards, Beverley, *Islamic Fundamentalism Since 1945* (London and New York: Routledge, 2014).

McDonagh, Philip, Kishan Manocha, John Neary and Lucia Vázquez Mendoza, *On the Significance of Religion for Global Diplomacy* (London and New York: Routledge, 2021).

Micklethwait, John and Adrian Wooldridge, *God is Back: How the Global Rise of Faith is Changing the World* (London: Penguin Books, 2010).

Moloney, Ed, *A Secret History of the IRA* (London: Penguin Books, 2002).

Moloney, Ed, *Paisley: From Demagogue to Democrat?* (Dublin: Poolbeg Press, 2008).

Moses, John A., *The Reluctant Revolutionary: Dietrich Bonhoeffer's Collision with Prusso-German History* (New York and Oxford: Berghahn Books, 2014).

Murphy, John A., *Ireland in the Twentieth Century* (Dublin: Gill and Macmillan, 1975).

Nye, Malory, *Religion: The Basics* (London and New York: Routledge, 2008) (2nd edn).

Christopher Partridge, ed., *The World's Religions* (Oxford: Lion, 2005).

Pettegree, Andrew, *Brand Luther: 1517, Printing, and the Making of the Reformation* (New York: Penguin Books, 2015).

Phillips, Elizabeth, *Political Theology* (London: T&T Clark International, 2012).

Rowland, Christopher, ed., *The Cambridge Companion to Liberation Theology* (Cambridge: Cambridge University Press, 1999).

Scott, Peter and William T. Cavanaugh, eds, *The Blackwell Companion to Political Theology* (Oxford: Blackwell, 2004).

Stanford, Peter, *Martin Luther: Catholic Dissident* (London: Hodder and Stoughton, 2017).

Tarnas, Richard, *The Passion of the Western Mind: Understanding the Ideas That Have Shaped Our World View* (London: Pimlico, 1991).

Thatcher, Margaret, *The Downing Street Years* (London: HarperCollins, 1993).

Wald, Kenneth D. and Allison Calhoun-Brown, *Religion and Politics in the United States* (New York and Oxford: Rowman and Littlefield Publishers, 2007) (5th edn).

Whyte, JH, *Church and State in Modern Ireland 1923–1979* (Dublin: Gill and Macmillan, 1980) (2nd edn).

Wilkinson, Alan, *Christian Socialism: Scott Holland to Tony Blair* (London: SCM Press, 1998).

Willey, David, *God's Politician: John Paul II and the Vatican* (London and Boston: Faber and Faber, 1993).

Woodhead, Linda, ed., *Religions in the Modern World: Traditions and Transformations* (London and New York: Routledge, 2009) (2nd edn).

Young, Hugo, *One of Us: A Biography of Margaret Thatcher* (London: Pan Books, 1990).